A Boy's Paradise

Life on a Turn-of-the-Century Farm
in the Upper Peninsula of Michigan

By Wilfred Nevue
With Susan M. Branting

Ten Sleep Press
Columbia, Maryland

A Boy's Paradise

ISBN 978-0-9859812-0-4

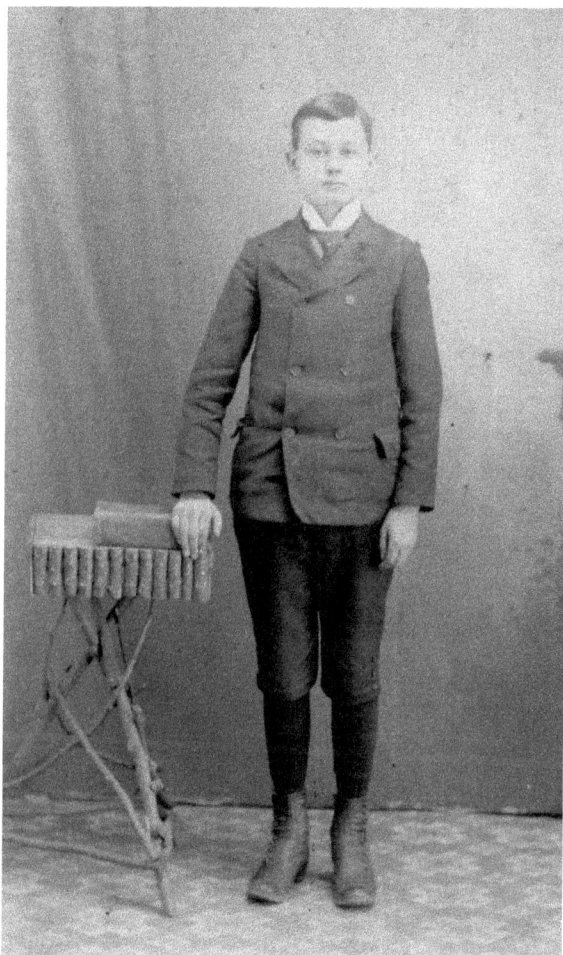

Wilfred "Pete Delongchamp" Nevue, age 14.

This book is dedicated to Wilfred Nevue's children,
for whom he wrote the original manuscript:
Lorraine, Eileen, Vivian, and Paul

Let's take a stroll just beyond the garden—all weeds now, but made sacred to me by the soft steps and toiling hands I loved—to the brow of the long down. The hot day cools rapidly as the sun pales above the maple and evergreen-covered hills to the north. To the east and west lay miles of hills and bluffs and the crushed remnants of the Huron Mountains: narrow valleys, tiny creeks, marshes, and plains.

Let's sit upon this rock—a pleasant spot to me, for I spent many hours dreaming here. Some of those dreams became realities: all of you, whom I so love.

This long, rocky and almost-barren down, then the narrow valley, and the hills beyond covered with pine, maple, birch, and all the evergreen indigenous to this region was once God's loveliest garden, now laid waste by the careless hand of man. The rocks and ridges once covered with rich black earth—now bare.

See, just below, almost at your feet. I gathered blackberries and the wild strawberries that grew among the hay in the damp bottom. And those stones along the fence? I helped to gather them so we could clear the land to plant the crops to fill the cellar. See that path just inside the fence? I drove the milk cows over it many times.

You sit entranced, but now you're turning cold, my dear. Take my hand as when you were a little girl and we shall stroll toward the setting sun, and when dusk, then darkness overtake us, under the stars we shall homeward go to return another evening where memory lingers.

—*Wilfred Nevue*

Table of Contents

Introduction

 In the late 1940s when he was in his 50s, my grandfather, Wilfred Nevue, began writing about his life in the Upper Peninsula of Michigan in the latter part of the previous century. He believed his younger self had lived a life that was quickly fading from the American experience, and he wished to capture it for his children. He was also greatly influenced by the Canadian novel *Maria Chapdelaine*, written in 1913 by the French writer Louis Hémon. In a letter about the book, he wrote, "Those French-Canadians are my people too. My home and much of the community life in which I grew were like that. Champion, and considerable of [sic] Marquette County, Michigan still has much of the tradition and customs that our ancestors brought from Quebec. I love it."

 I have tried to stay loyal to his style while cleaning up confusing or awkward constructions and correcting grammar and punctuation. I added details from other autobiographical documents and stories he wrote, as well as an introduction to each section. The result, I hope, is more readable without straying from the voice and intent of the original text.

—Susan M. Branting
Columbia, Maryland

1

Down from Quebec

J ean Louis Delongchamp[1] and his younger brother Maxime[2] arrived in the Upper Peninsula of Michigan about 1860 and purchased a farm a mile and a half north of the small town of Champion in Marquette County.

On February 2, 1867, Jean Louis, then twenty seven, married sixteen-year-old Celina Blais in St. Paul's Church in Negaunee, Michigan. Born in Canada on January 1, 1851, Celina had settled in Negaunee with her father, Jean Blais, and her mother, Zoe, as well as many brothers and sisters.

In 1868, Celina gave birth to their first child and named her Celina. Five more children followed: John, Alfred, Mary Nellie, Eloise, and Delima.[3]

Just 16 years after their marriage, Jean Louis died at age forty three, leaving his thirty-two-year-old wife with five children between the ages of six and sixteen. The next year, in 1884, the widow married Maxime, who took over the farm and his brother's place in rearing the children.

---

[1] Born in the province of Quebec in 1840.
[2] Born in the province of Quebec in 1847. Jean Louis and Maxime's parents were Jean Louis Delongchamp and Marguerite Trudel.
[3] Delima probably died at birth or in infancy.

3

Grandmother Celina with her first husband, Jean Louis, and
their oldest child (Wilfred's mother) Celina and baby John.

The daughter Celina was just 16 when her father died, and within two years she had taken up with Wilfred Nevue,[4] who may

---

[4] There is no information about this man; however, the names "Wilfred" and "Nevue" are in records in Quebec, Canada. His son, the author, wrote that the name had been spelled Neveaux but that he did not know when or why the spelling was changed.

have been employed by a lumber company. Theirs was a shotgun wedding: after Celina became pregnant, Wilfred Nevue was forced to marry her.

Wilfred's parents: Wilfred Nevue and Celina Delongchamp.

Their son, Wilfred Nevue, was born April 19, 1886, in Republic, Michigan. For reasons that are unclear, he was called Peter Delongchamp at home, though at least some of his school records listed him as Wilfred Nevue. When he was six months old, his father deserted him and his mother, and they were taken into the home of his stepgrandfather, Maxime,[5] and grandmother, Celina.

Wilfred (center, sitting) surrounded by his aunts, uncles (standing and left) and cousins (two girls at right).

The last time Peter saw his mother was at three years of age when she was confined to Traverse City State Hospital. She was 21

---

[5] Technically his great uncle, but Wilfred refers to him in this book as his grandfather or stepgrandfather.

and would stay in the mental institution until her death at the age of 28. In a report of her death many years later, a hospital official noted, "She appeared to be suffering from manic depressive psychosis. As the records show, she had a fairly long period of elation followed by depression. It was apparently during this depression that her health gradually failed and she died July 2, 1896."

Wilfred, raised by his grandparents, labored from his earliest years to contribute to the survival of the household while attending Champion public schools. His mother's two brothers treated him cruelly, and his stepgrandfather worked him hard, but his affection for his grandmother, whom he called "a saint," sustained him, as is obvious in the stories he chose to tell about his youth.

.

Delongchamp/Blais/Nevue

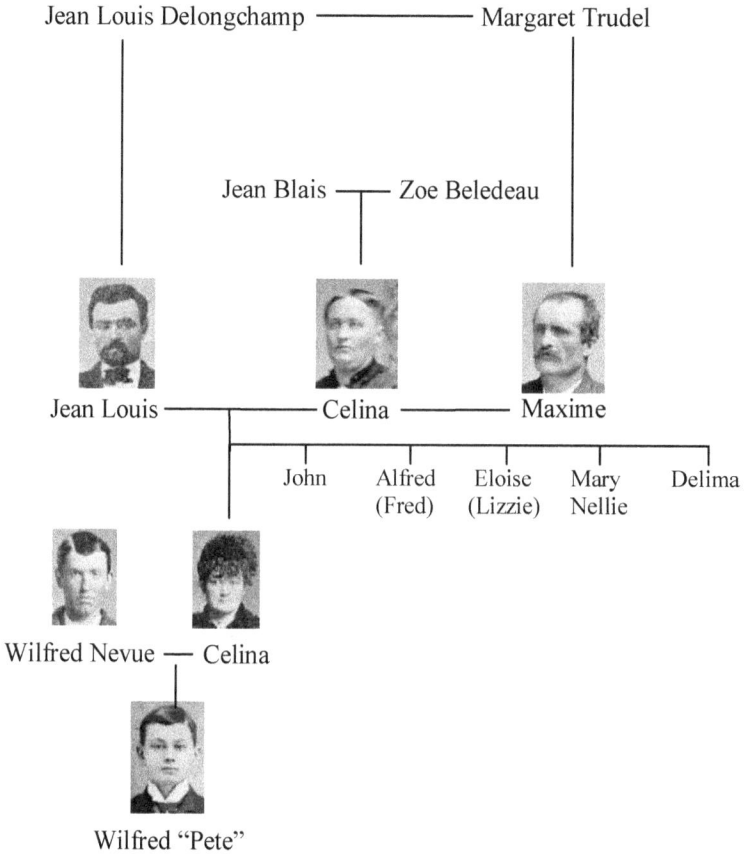

Jean Louis Delongchamp ——————— Margaret Trudel

Jean Blais —— Zoe Beledeau

Jean Louis ——————— Celina ——————— Maxime

| | John | Alfred (Fred) | Eloise (Lizzie) | Mary Nellie | Delima |

Wilfred Nevue —— Celina

Wilfred "Pete"

Home

Wilfred grew up well before television and radio, and though electricity was gaining in the cities, it was not available in the rough farm where he lived. Instead, his days were filled with chores and school, from well before dawn to the early evening when he fell into his straw bed exhausted. Almost everything his family ate and wore had to be grown, processed, or fabricated—from the wool socks on their feet to the butter they spread on their homemade bread.

Habitants

About 400 people were spread over the five square miles of western Marquette County where Champion and the town of Beacon lay. The area was swampy and full of boulders. The slopes, mostly cleared of trees, were rocky and eroded. Nearly all the forest within horse-team distance had been consumed for building the community—houses, stores, roads, and bridges—as well as for making charcoal and for fuel. Buildings of all kinds—houses, barns, outhouses, sheds, and little stores were scattered haphazardly, as though they had been flung by a giant sower.[6]

The towns were founded by mining companies, and mines dotted the area. Champion boasted one of the first iron smelting furnaces in the Great Lakes region. All the land on which the buildings stood belonged to a mining company—first Champion Iron Mining Company and then Oliver Iron Mining Company—which leased the land to the private building owners.

Besides iron mining, the abundance of cedar, spruce, and tamarack in the valley to the north and Norway (red) and white

---

[6] Someone who scatters seeds by hand. See the chapter "Hard Rocks and Furrow Lines."

pine on the Huron Mountains attracted some settlers and were important to the timber industry.

Woodcutters with a load of pulpwood.

Nearly all the settlers—mostly French Canadian, Cornish, Finnish, Swedish, and Irish—were immigrants. I recall only two Italian, three German, and one Jewish family. The French Canadian and Cornish men were most interested in any work involving timber; nearly all the rest were miners, railroad section-workers, or small-business owners. The few who were interested in the gruel- ing, hard work of farming were French Canadian *habitants*— farmers. For generations their ancestors had been *habitants* in

Quebec Province, Canada. Working in *la terre*[7] was their lives; but as much as the French Canadians in Marquette County wanted to be *habitants* and work *la terre* for a living, they were often greatly frustrated. Many of them attempted to establish homes on farms only to abandon the projects as hopeless in the inhospitable land.

My home was one that, while genuinely backwoods, was quite self-sustaining. We had more than any other pioneer family, for we raised a few pigs and brined and salted the pork, butchered our beef in early winter, raised potatoes, turnips, and rutabagas in small patches among the stumps in newly cleared rocky ground, and harvested peas and a small amount of wheat, which we hauled thirty miles to have ground in a small water-powered mill on Dead River near Marquette.

Grandmother had a bit of a garden in which she raised green onions, carrots, string beans, and cabbages. She tried persistently to raise cucumbers, tomatoes, and sweet corn but with little success—they usually froze before maturing, as the growing season was too short.

For our winter fruits, we had usually abundant dried prunes, peaches, pears, and apples that we bought in the little towns' stores, as well as wild fruit.

---

[7] The earth.

When the days began to warm at the start of spring, we watched anxiously for the frost to pass early enough to allow the blossoms of the wild fruit to survive and mature.

Wild raspberries and blackberries grew among the rocks in the fences and the rock piles in the fields. They grew along the abandoned railroads and about the remains of the old iron mines. We found wild strawberries in the hay fields and meadows and blueberries among the stumps. I climbed the willowy branches of the pincherry tree for the dainty clustered cherries. The juice of the chokecherries made our wine. Carelessly, I ventured into the soft and sinky bog surrounding the little lake to gather the few quarts of small cranberries. I also gathered hazelnuts from the hazelnut bushes for Grandmother's delicious cookies and cakes.

Smudge Pots and Butter Churns

W hoever selected the site for the house must have come from a warm climate, because the house stood on the north side of a thick grove of large maples.

Delongchamp farm house.

The house was quite large, but it was more attractive than comfortable, having been constructed of one layer of siding and a thin plastered wall. It had been built for the superintendent of the small local mines, though he lived in it only one season.

The main house consisted of a parlor, living room, bedroom, and kitchen downstairs, and a single large room upstairs.

Whenever anyone went upstairs, he pushed the door with his head, got through, and then usually let the door slam with a bang. In summer, the room was occupied by our one or two hired men, my two uncles, and myself. It was also used as a storeroom for wheat and *poise*.[8] After the men left for the winter's work in the logging camps,[9] the room was all mine.

During the short summer, that upstairs room was not pleasant to sleep in because screens were not in common use and the mosquitoes were very annoying.

The most effective method for fighting mosquitoes was with smoke smudges. To make a smudge, we put damp earth in the bottom of a leaky, old, tin pail, then filled the container with dry chips and twigs which we set on fire. After the fire was burning well, we covered it with damp, packed leaves to smother the flames. The smoke from the embers filled the room and drove the mosquitoes outside or to the corners. The smudge had to be kept

---

[8] Peas, a major crop on the farm.

[9] Because the land could not be farmed in the winter, the men earned money cutting the virgin forests for lumber companies. They worked in the winter because the huge logs could only be moved on ice-covered roads using horse-drawn sleds.

going or the pests would come right back to hum and sting. Sometimes the mosquitoes were so thick, every room in use had its own smudge.

The final two or three years that I slept in that bedroom were a little better because Grandmother tacked cheesecloth over the windows. That helped some, but the cheesecloth tore easily, so many mosquitoes came in anyway. Imagine the discomfort of covering one's head to sleep in the hot, humid summer!

In contrast to the heat of mid-summer was the intense cold of winter. The room was heated by a short length of tin stove pipe that rose through the floor from the big boxstove downstairs, but in such a large room, that bit of heat was not much good.

While lying in bed I had to rely on the heat of my body and the warmth of my breath. I had ample bed covers, including woolen blankets, Grandmother's handmade quilts, and two large buffalo robes. I was well covered, but the layer of straw over the bed slats and a blue cotton sheet were not enough bedding underneath my body. As the winter grew colder, I spread one of the buffalo robes under me. Sometimes in desperation, I spread one of the buffalo robes on the floor and lay there.

My grandparents occupied the only downstairs bedroom. It could be kept reasonably warm in winter, and, being in the shade of the maple trees, it was comfortable in summer. My two aunts slept in the living room until they married and left home.

The parlor was the smaller of the two other rooms in the house. The furniture there consisted of a settee, several cane-bottomed chairs, and an antique Estey organ.[10] My aunts played simple tunes on the organ, and Grandmother picked out very simple melodies that entranced me. A few enlarged family portraits on the walls reminded us of the departed. Also on the walls hung two colored, hand-needled mottoes Grandmother had stitched. A chandelier, lit by a kerosene lamp, hung from the center of the ceiling. I was fascinated by the glittering colors of the dangling crystals. The entire floor was covered by a red rug. Grandmother spread a layer of straw under the rug every spring to make the footing soft and also to make the floor pleasant to sit on. But if people had smoked cigarettes as they do now,[11] the whole thing would have made excellent kindling for starting a disastrous fire. A big brass-faced clock hung on the wall.

The living room was quite large. The stairway, with a closet under it, ran along the wall between the living room and the parlor. At one side stood a drop-leaf table and, near the window, Grand-

---

[10] The Estey Organ Company, based in Brattleboro, Vermont, was founded in 1846 by Jacob Estey, a plumber experienced in making lead pipes and copper pumps. Until 1901, it specialized in reed organs—the type in Wilfred's home—and had built around a half million by the time it closed in 1960.

[11] This manuscript was written in the 1950s–1960s when a large number of Americans smoked, including Wilfred.

20

mother's flower stand of curved wooden shelves arranged like stair steps.

Grandmother loved potted plants, and I loved them too, because we cared for them together. Each evening when the fire began to die, we covered the plants with paper or cloth and placed them in a corner away from the frosted windows. The next morning, if the weather was not too cold, we set the pots on the shelves; however, all of our care was not sufficient to bring them through the winter without some of them freezing in the pots. It took the plants much of the following summer to revive.

A large iron boxstove, about four feet long and waist high, heated the house. Wood for it was cut about two feet long. Maple and birch trees provided the best wood. Soft wood, mostly dead pine and dry cedar, was kept for kindling and whittling, or to make quick fires in summer. The tin stovepipe that extended upward through the ceiling into my bedroom entered the chimney by means of an elbow. A tin drum, through which the pipe passed, protected the ceiling from burning.

Until about the time that I entered high school, I did not have much to do with cutting wood in the forests and hauling it to the woodshed; but from a very early age, I sawed and split wood once it was brought to the house. In summer, I carried the "small split," or branch wood, in my arms. In winter, I used a homemade sled to haul all the wood so I could do so all at one time, to avoid opening the door too much. The kitchen stove wood was stacked in a large box. The boxstove wood was piled in a rick between two upright boards.

Regardless of the cold and long winter days, we managed to be comfortably warm—except our feet and legs. The stove sometimes got red hot. I stood as near as possible to the red hot sides until my shins began to feel like they were roasting, then I turned around like meat on a barbecue. I have always enjoyed roasting my legs near a good wood fire.

The living room floor was covered with thick round or oval cloth rugs that Grandmother hand-braided. To make the rugs, she saved and sorted all kinds of cloth, putting aside wool for quilts and cotton for rugs. Never one to waste time or material, whenever she had a few moments to relax from more arduous work, she sat down with her basket of rags. The rags were torn or cut into strips about an inch wide and tied end-to-end regardless of their color. The long strips were then braided—three strips to a braid. She began a rug in the middle, sewing the edges of the braids together with fine stitches. Whenever anyone sat near a rug, he was certain to heel it closer, for it was so much more comfortable than the cold floor.

Along the north end of the house, was a lean-to divided into a kitchen and a storeroom. The storeroom also contained a milk house and an icehouse and was used as a summer kitchen.

The big kitchen, where Grandmother cooked for the family and the few men who boarded with us, was equipped with a large farmer stove, a long table made of boards, a spacious built-in cupboard, and a wooden sink in one corner. The sink and a hand pump were over a well that had been dug when the house was built, but the water was polluted. I never saw the pump operated, and the well water was used only on the plants and the garden.

The floor of the milk house was made of stone and the walls were insulated with sawdust. Broad shelves extended along the walls. On those shelves Grandmother placed her canned fruit, pickled beets, cucumber pickles (which she made about every third year), eggs, milk, cream, butter, salt pork, and leftovers. In one corner we had one or two barrels of brined pork. When we had venison in summer, it was kept iced in barrels.

The milk was strained and poured into earthen bowls and kept in the milk house until the cream formed thick layers on top, after which the cream was skimmed and gathered in a crock until there was enough to make butter.

Saturday was butter-churning day. When Grandmother decided to make butter, she carried the cream to the bench near the stove. In winter the cream did not sour enough and in summer it soured too much. However, Grandmother's good butter was in demand in the community.

Grandmother chose one of three methods to churn butter, depending on the amount of cream.

If there were only two or three quarts of cream, she poured it into a round-bottomed bowl and agitated it by going round and round with her right hand, fingers spread. I remember well how she

23

placed a bowl of cream between her knees and pressed it there as she churned.

If there were two or three gallons of cream, I made the butter using an upright churn, usually doing the job after dark. The churn consisted of a tall earthenware crock with a wooden lid through which passed a wooden handle. The cream was agitated by the paddle at the end of the handle as it went up and down. At each stroke, I turned the handle slightly.

In summer, when there was too much cream for either of the first two methods, we used a box-like churn. The box stood on four legs and was about eighteen inches square and two feet high. A crank attached to a shaft turned a four-paddled agitator inside the box.

After the cream turned to butter in the churn, Grandmother lifted the mass and pressed out as much water and whey as she could. Then the real work began. She placed a half-pound chunk of butter in her outstretched left hand, then with her right hand held at arm's length she slapped it hard, then flipped the chunk over and slapped that side, repeating this over and over. How the whey flew! When the butter was as free from whey as she could make it, she squeezed salt into it. At intervals she tasted a pinch of butter to test its salinity. When it was to her taste, each chunk was carefully pressed into a crock and then stored in the milk house. Sometimes she sold some butter in small bowls or crocks. If she sold it by the pound, she beat the butter into pound chunks and made designs on the top with a knife. While school was in session, I delivered the surplus butter to customers on my way to school. In summer we delivered it on our way to church.

A shallow cellar extended under the main part of the house; we had to stoop to walk in it. Here we stored our *pattat*,[12] turnips, and other vegetables. After the wild berries were no longer available, we always had at least one barrel of apples at the foot of the cellar stairs. When the temperature was very low, we covered our food with straw, bags, and sometimes blankets from the barn. Nearly every winter some of our *pattat* frosted, and when that happened, we ate sweet Irish *pattat*, but they did not taste very good. The cellar had been built into solid rock, so nearly every spring when the snow melted, it flooded and everything had to be carried out.

In summer, all the water for cooking and other household uses was hauled in barrels from a well near the barn on a jumper, which was a low contraption on wooden runners. In winter, after the wells froze solid, we either lugged water from a large open-pit iron mine or melted snow in our wash boilers. In summer, the water barrels stayed out of doors, but in winter they had to be in the house. During warm weather, two barrels gathered rain water from spouts on the roof. Those rain barrels were good breeding pools for mosquitoes.

---

[12] French Canadian for potatoes.

25

Near the house stood the long, flat-roofed wood-and-buggy shed against which the privy stood.

In winter, snow drifted in banks higher than the shed's roof, and the board fence about the premises disappeared, so that we did not pass through the gates—we just walked over the fences.

Soap-making was another task Grandmother had to fit into her busy days. It was a long, slow process that started with the first frost in the fall and continued through the balmy days of spring. To make soap, we needed lye, fat, and rosin or pitch.[13]

We made the lye from ashes. Whoever cleaned the boxstove and the farmer stove scooped out the ashes and dumped them into some old pickle barrels in the woodshed. In spring, the snow on the roofs melted and filled the barrels of ash. A spout was poked into the bottom side of the barrel to drain the water which, as it trickled through the ashes, made four or five gallons of weak lye.

The fat came from our animals. When the autumn frosts set in, we always butchered two or three pigs and, a little later, a cow or steer. A week before Christmas, we slaughtered another steer. All the entrail fat of the pigs was rendered into lard, but the stringy, inedible parts and the tallow from the beef were packed into whisky barrels or beer kegs—given to us by Champion's saloon owner— and stored in the buggy shed.

---

[13] Rosin consists of small dry chunks of gum pried from spruce trees; the pitch came from slicing blisters from balsam trees.

Grandmother strained the weak lye-water to clean it, then boiled it so the water evaporated. To test the lye's strength, she occasionally dropped a potato into it. If the potato floated, the lye was strong enough.

Next, Grandmother chopped the tallow and hog fat into small chunks and boiled the mess slowly, then filtered out the clear fat from the stringy waste. The clear fat, the lye, and the rosin, or pitch, were cooked slowly over a big fire outdoors until the water evaporated and the mixture condensed. She scooped some out, cooked it further on the farmer stove, and poured the soap into pans to cool and harden. Anything that didn't harden was used in water for clothes boiling (bar soap was used on the washboard), mopping the floor, and similar purposes. Grandmother was an artist at making soap.

Another task that took up much of Grandmother's time was putting to use the wool from the sheep we raised. I would carry an armful of fluffy white wool from the shed and place it in a basket near where Grandmother sat in her rocking chair by the boxstove. Most of the wool was white, but sometimes a black sheep was born. We saved their wool to make work clothes.

Pushing and pulling chunks of wool between two antique cards that she had brought with her from Montreal, she rolled it into little balls that she could spin into yarn on her good spinning wheel.

The best time to spin wool into yarn was after supper, when there were few interruptions, for spinning yarn took concentration.

Grandmother often spun deep into the night. The product of this labor she knitted fast and skillfully using four long needles into socks, mittens, toques,[14] and scarves for the use of the members of our household and for sale to the lumberjacks. The finest ones, though—they were for me.

---

[14] A stocking cap or simple wool hat without bill or ear flaps.

Superstitions

Because we had the most modern farming equipment around, my grandfather[15] and I frequently traveled to other farms to rent our threshing outfit to the French Canadian farmers. During threshing season, we stayed at their homes, and it was there that I learned many French Canadian *contes*[16] and superstitions.

The moon was the most influential thing in our lives, and the most vital effect of the moon was on unborn children and their births. Parents worried and expressed their fears and distress. If a child was conceived or born during the dark of the moon, it might be seriously affected in its sight, hearing, speech, or mind; it might be clubfooted. Prospective mothers prayed for delivery when the moon was full.

On Christmas Eve, the animals talked to each other and kneeled at midnight. Once I suggested going to the barn to witness this marvelous event, but I was told that the cattle would not kneel in the presence of a person and to disturb them was an awful sin.

---

[15] His stepgrandfather, Maxime.
[16] Tales.

On New Year's Eve, we listened intently for the howls of the *lou garou*.[17] It was dangerous to be out, but that was the particular night when French Canadians celebrate most. The harsh, loud wind was sometimes imagined to be wolf howls. When I went to town and returned home at night in the winter, I dreaded the *lou garou*.

I was fully taken in by this one superstition: if a cow's udder was injured and the milk was bloody, we knew a snake had sucked the udder, and the snake always did this at night. I did everything possible to find that snake but, of course, like the *lou garou*, it never existed. The only snakes I ever saw were little green garter snakes.

My favorite superstition was spitting on an angleworm after it was impaled on a fishhook. I thoroughly believed in it and, of course, I was faithful to the superstition. I caught some nice trout that way ....

I was raised in a very religious and devout Catholic home. An Italian family with whom we were friendly lived on top of the hill near the old Champion furnace.[18] One fall morning when we were driving to church up in Beacon, we saw that the Italian family was building a wood shed of poplar poles. Stepgrandfather gasped and stopped the wagon team. He called the Italian man out and severely

---

[17] Werewolf.

[18] A large, stone furnace in which charcoal was burned to extract iron from ore.

30

castigated him for building anything with poplar poles. He said that the cross on which Christ was crucified was made of the same kind of poplar and that to build anything with poplar would bring calamity on everybody around. Grandfather and Joe the Italian ceased to be good friends. One of the daughters had become crippled (probably polio), and her illness was blamed on the poplar pole shed.

We had a number of remedies for illnesses. For sores, injuries, and all kinds of aches, the best salve was wild garlic juice mixed with tallow. Skunk grease was an excellent salve as well, but there was one remedy that my grandparents and I never fell for. We had the only flock of sheep that I ever knew of far and wide. For some French Canadians, our sheep provided free medicine for colds, sore throats, and inflammation of the bowels (probably appendicitis). Men and women came to our farm to gather fresh sheep droppings—especially of lambs or ewes. They boiled them into a black juice, added sugar, and then boiled the juice into a thick syrup to drink. It was known to be a very potent medicine.

In those days, the most common and enjoyed entertainment was the show-troops that came to town to sell Indian medicines. Three or four such troops came each winter. The shows were in town or at the company hall near the Champion mine. The hall was always crowded—mostly with French Canadians, for they were perfect suckers and most easily duped.

Grandmother

Married at 16, widowed at 32 with five children, Celina Delongchamp was just 36 when her grandson Wilfred was born. Plump and dark-haired, she was never still. Even sitting in her rocking chair by the boxstove was a time for braiding rugs, carding wool, and sewing. She and her daughters stitched patch-quilts and did fancy bits of cooking. They visited and entertained rarely, although her home was sometimes a meeting place for quilting parties, maple-sugar parties, and other get-togethers. Among the approximately 50 Canadian families in the area, she was the only person with enough education to write letters, for herself and others, and to read the Montreal newspaper. In the later years of his life, Wilfred looked back on his time with her as a boy's paradise, for she gave him something no one else ever did—a love that was deep and without reservation.

Grandmother and her second husband, Maxime.

The Spectacle Man

Grandmother needed spectacles, but to get a pair she would have to go to Ishpeming, Negaunee, or Marquette—sixteen to thirty miles—a long way in a buggy. And money was scarce. So Grandmother kept putting the matter off, waiting to save enough money. I pledged that the first money I earned would be spent for that purpose, and at last I was able to help.

I had worked at the North Mine all summer and earned forty-five dollars. Having collected my wages the day before school opened in September, I was elated to give the check to Grandmother, so she could go to one of the cities to buy spectacles.

When I gave Grandmother my check, she happily told me that a spectacle man—a real doctor—had come to Champion. He advertised that he was good and reliable and came from Montreal; he knew the nationality of his prospective customers. She showed me his card, which a well-meaning friend had given to her at the man's request.

Yes sir, he was a good spectacle man—it said so on the card.

After dinner Grandmother and I rode the buckboard to town, both of us happy. The buckboard bumped over rocks and the corduroy road. The old mare's tail swished the flies.

Grandmother cashed the check at the grocery store and we went to see the spectacle man. His hands churned and he was ultra-graciousness. I felt uncomfortable with his manner, but Grandmother had forty-five dollars and needed spectacles.

He placed a pair of his glasses before her eyes and pressed them into place on her nose. He simulated looking through the lenses. He raised them to the light. He slid behind her to move the spectacles up and down while he covetously looked over Grandmother's shoulder at those dear hands holding the precious money. I think he licked his lips. He blew on the lenses and wiped them with his dirty handkerchief. He touched the back of her head; I was repelled. He held the glasses in the line of her vision.

"How much?" Grandmother asked. She did not catch my frown of disapproval.

"To you—Canadian—special price—special price."

Grandmother smiled. The man practically drooled as she unfolded the crisp bills.

"Twenty-two dollars. Twenty-two dollars," he said.

Grandmother's shoulders sagged as she glanced at me. But, she needed spectacles. Hesitantly she handed that man twenty-two dollars, and as he tightened his fingers about the cash, he adjusted the steel frame and bows. Then he walked across the room and held up a paper with lettering on it. Grandmother was shocked and bewildered—she could not read the print.

"You see," said the man slyly, "Those are near lenses. They are to read. Now you need spectacles to see far."

Grandmother squeezed the remaining bills and pressed her hand to her lap. She looked up at me inquiringly. Did I approve? But I said nothing—she needed spectacles.

The man fitted a pair of thick-lensed glasses over the first pair and pressed lightly. Grandmother's head jerked back. He stepped across the room and held up a card. Yes! Grandmother could read the print. She smiled at me, two pairs of ill-fitting glasses on her nose. I was shocked. Mentally I protested. But again I said nothing. Grandmother needed spectacles.

"How much?" asked Grandmother as she glanced at the bills in her open hand.

"Just twenty-two dollars. A bargain. A bargain."

She smoothed the bills on her lap, then handed all but one dollar of my hard-earned summer wages to the "doctor."

I would have worked months, years, any length of time, to earn money to buy glasses for Grandmother.

The man expounded on the bargain. He wrapped the glasses in a cloth and handed them to Grandmother along with his card with a Montreal address—in French.

Grandmother was very happy as she and I rode home in the buckboard.

Watching Grandmother as she tried to accustom herself to those glasses distressed me. She tried to get along with them, then

37

without them. She pressed them into position, rubbed the bridge of her nose and the backs of her ears. She held them in place with one hand while she struggled to work with the other. She tried to get along with one pair. She blinked and wiped her eyes with the corner of her apron.

But Grandmother had confidence in those glasses. They had to be good. The doctor from Montreal said so.

One day, while Grandmother was inspecting the nest of a turkey-hen to see if any of the chicks had hatched, she neglected to remove the glasses. When she pushed her hand under the hen, the bird flapped its wings in Grandmother's face, flinging the outer glasses to the floor and breaking them.

Getting a replacement would be easy—the "doctor" from Montreal had said so. But Grandmother needed another twenty-two dollars. Finally, by saving small amounts of money from selling butter and from knitting stockings and mittens for the men in the lumber camps and shanties, she had enough. She took the spectacle man's card from her little treasure box.

Carefully packaging the broken glasses, she mailed them—registered—to the man's address in Montreal. She included a nice letter in her best French and a money-order for twenty-two dollars.

Then Grandmother waited. Confidently, she waited.

And a letter did come and a package, too—the letter she had written and the money-order and the package with the broken spectacles.

Christmas Stockings

hristmas Eve. The green curtains had been drawn, softening the cold from the thickly frosted windows. The living room was soothingly warm with the heat from the boxstove, near which Grandmother rocked, happily knitting.

I had heard about Santa Claus from my young friends, but nothing had occurred to convince me he was real. Grandmother eyed me silently as I slipped slyly about the room.

Bed time was near, so I went to the clothes basket in the closet under the stairway and dug out two of my long, black, woolen stockings. In those days, boys wore stockings that extended above their knees. I carefully hung the stockings from the small brass hooks screwed into the bottom of the clock, stretched them down, then went to Grandmother. I knelt at her side with my elbows in her lap and said my prayers. We kissed. I rushed upstairs to my buffalo-robe bed.

Grandmother had been awake for some time when she called up to my room to wake me on Christmas morning. The living room and the kitchen were comfortably warm, and Grandmother was preparing breakfast. As I descended the stairs, I saw Grandmother watching me through the kitchen door. The feet of my hanging stockings bulged. I smiled at Grandmother, unhooked the stockings. I was in ecstasy.

Jamming my hand into a stocking, I felt something round and smooth. Pulling out the object, I beheld, to my great joy, a beautiful orange. I felt its coolness, held it to my nose, and pressed it with my tongue. I held it high for Grandmother to see. She beamed. I ran to her and placed the orange in her hand, then ran back to the stocking. Next, out came a small, wrapped, crisp package. I opened it and found a few of Grandmother's delicious cookies. Grandmother eyed me closely. Her eyes twinkled. I fingered the foot of the stocking and felt small, round, hard objects. Reaching in, I drew out a handful of hazelnuts—hazelnuts that I had gathered and hulled.

The utensils and the stove lids clinked.

There were soft steps about the kitchen.

Santa Claus had come.

La Fête du Jour de L'An

Throughout the year, whatever work Grandmother and I did together added something to our preparation for the great *Fête du Jour de L'An*,[19] which was more important to the French Canadians than was Christmas. It was also Grandmother's birthday.

Our deepest concern was our turkeys—two hens and a gobbler. We tended them diligently, for as spring advanced, the hens would lay their speckled eggs in nests hidden in the remnants of the straw stacks, in the dark nooks in the barns, or in the thick bushes.

I assumed the assignment of watching those turkey hens and looking for their eggs. While I was at school, Grandmother gathered the eggs in her apron, and when the hens began to set, she placed thirteen eggs under each hen.

One spring we experienced a near calamity. One of our turkey-hens died. The other hen eluded us and laid her eggs in a nest in the bushes. We searched and watched but could not find her nest. One day, as Grandmother and I were working in her garden, we were surprised to see the hen with her little brood near the house.

---

[19] New Year's Day festival.

41

She had seven chicks. We were delighted. Now we would have turkey for *La Fête du Jour de L'An*.

That evening, before the hen could sneak to her hideout, we cornered her, and, with a stout cord, tethered her to a stake by the door of the little brood house. In that manner the hen was kept under surveillance. But with the passing days, the chicks became too large to stay with their mother while she was fastened to a stake. Grandmother, believing the hen had abandoned her wandering ways, removed the tether and freed the hen. For several days the hen and her brood returned to the little brood house, and every evening Grandmother closed and fastened the door to protect them from predators.

One evening, the hen and her seven chicks did not return from their day's wandering. We were greatly apprehensive. Day after day I hunted and watched for our turkeys, and Grandmother joined me in the search when she could spare moments from her household duties. Evenings I went to the highest places from which I hoped to spot our precious turkeys.

Despondent, we accepted the loss of our turkeys. If the neighbors had had turkeys, this disaster would not have been so depressing. We had the gobbler, but we needed more than one bird for the great feast. Finally we resigned ourselves to chicken. Oh, my.

The fall wore on, and threshing was almost finished. The nights were cold and the chickens snuggled more and more closely on the roosts. The trees were almost bare of their gorgeously colored leaves. Finally, it was the last day of threshing. All that remained in the fields were a few sheaves near the western fence at the edge of the woods. One more wagon load. I held the slack lines while the men filled the wagon's rack.[20] The team pulled the wagon from shock to shock.[21] The men hurriedly pitched the sheaves to the top of the growing load. As I drove, watching the ground, I suddenly noticed a turkey hurrying in the stubble, heading directly toward the barn. What was I seeing? Excitedly I called my grandfather, the loader. He counted, jabbing his fork. "One, two, three, four, five, six, seven, eight!"

"Giddap!" I slapped the lines across the horses' backs. The load rocked and the wagon bumped. We watched the turkeys as they neared the barn, gathering momentum and not deviating one bit from their straight course, their heads oscillating in unison. They disappeared through the barnyard gate. Loading the few remaining sheaves seemed to take a long time—I wanted to hurry to the barn; I wanted to see those turkeys. No wandering child was ever more welcome home than those turkeys. Where had they been? How had they escaped the foxes and the weasels? With the last sheaves on the load, we were off to the barn.

---

[20] A wooden frame on the back of the wagon.
[21] The wheat was gathered and tied into sheaves. A "shock" is a pile of sheaves.

I stood on the load to look over the barn fence, leaning sideways to see beyond of the straw piles. I lost my balance—almost falling forward onto the horses. I got my balance and jerked the lines to urge the horses. The team entered the barnyard gate where I saw, between cattle legs, eight turkeys grouped near a straw stack. The gobbler, with his head thrust back, strutted before them, his big hanging wattle brilliant red. Never had I seen such beautiful turkeys. I threw the lines to one side, slid down the load, and walked to the flock. The gobbler looked so pompous. Ecstatic, I ran to the house.

"*Grand'mere!*" I called to Grandmother. "The turkeys, the turkeys! They're here!" I grabbed her hand and we ran to the barn. She was so happy. We hugged.

Then Grandmother leaned toward the birds and pointed at the hen. There was something peculiar about one of her wings.

I cornered the hen, caught her, and held her up. Grandmother smoothed her fingers under the left wing. The long feathers of that wing had been cropped. In fact, the left wings of all the turkeys had been cropped to prevent them from flying, probably from over an enclosure.

Because of the direction from which the wandering turkeys had come, we knew well which of our neighbors had imprisoned them. But, oh joy! Our turkeys had come home!

The freezing soil and flecks of snow heralded the approaching New Year. Turkeys were selected for fattening and confined in a barnyard pen where they were amply fed with freshly harvested barley.

One weekend in late November, the men came back from the lumber camp to slaughter a cow and one or two pigs. The quarters were hung from rafters or beams, or laid on the summer kitchen table. The best cuts would be set aside to be roasted for the feast.

The day before *La Fête du Jour de L'An*, the men came home again. The deep snow, which had drifted across the roads, must not interfere with the celebration! They snow-plowed the road to town to make it passable for the hay riders in their cutters and sleighs. The water barrels were refilled. The lamps and the lanterns were cleaned and filled with kerosene.

Finally the day before the *fête* arrived, and we began the exciting preparations.

Morning. A fire cracked in the big boxstove. The spinning wheel sat in a corner of the room. In the kitchen, the six-lid farmer stove with its spacious box oven. The yellow-flamed lamp bracketed to the wall lit the kitchen as Grandmother hummed softly.

Warmly clothed and with a small lantern swinging, I rushed into the bitterly cold and penetrating wind. Through the snow, over the fences and drifts, I hurried to the steamy barn. I forked the straw from the mow, poked down the hay from the loft, and stuffed the mangers. The huddled pigs grunted in the dark and the roosting hens and turkeys pulled their heads from under their wings and thrust them back again.

I surveyed my charges. All was well. Back to the house to my breakfast of warm French pancakes, maple syrup, and fried brined pork. The lights began to pencil around the green curtains, and when Grandmother raised them, Jack Frost displayed his artistry. The sunlight glistened on the crusted snow.

Immediately after breakfast, I finished the morning chores in the barn, then used my handmade wooden sleigh to haul in the day's wood, ricking it high behind the stoves in the kitchen and living room so the house could be kept warm well into the night. Late in the day I hitched the old mare to the wooden bobsled and slipped through the fields and over the ridge to the Dalliba pit.[22] I filled the bobsled's two barrels with water from holes chipped through the thick ice. In the afternoon, the cattle would travel over the same broken trail for their daily watering.

All the remaining time not necessary for chores I spent helping Grandmother prepare for the great day. She baked cookies, cakes, and pies. From the barrel in the cellar, she took big apples and polished them. The red tablecloths were ironed. The iron-case cutlery was polished and shined for the guests. Some days before, I had gotten the well-fleshed turkeys from the barn, now they were plucked and dressed, ready for roasting.

---

[22] The water-filled remains of an abandoned open-pit mine called the Dalliba mine.

When *la Jour de l'An* finally arrived, the workload eased. Almost everything was ready: the frosted cakes, the crumbly cookies in glass jars, and pies tempting on the shelves of the wall cupboard, a basket of shiny apples, the garlic-scented pork roast, the plump-breasted turkeys waiting for the box oven.

As evening came, we saw the fine snow swishing over the fields and the horizon darkening in the east.

The lamps were lit and Grandmother and I waited for the men to return. Suddenly, we heard an explosion of men's voices outside the door accompanied by the hard stamping of feet to shake off the snow, the muffled slap of mittened hands, the slamming of the door.

Supper was ready. On the long table, Grandmother had heaped a plate with broad, thick slices of her homemade bread. On the farmer stove, a kettle of delicious *soupe de pois*[23] simmered. And, too, there were the big hot *pattat*. From the cold summer kitchen, I brought an earthen bowl filled with chunks of cold, boiled brined pork.

After dinner and when Grandmother and I had washed the dishes, we joined the men in the living room to await the round of revelers. We heard the singing and laughing men coming in their sleighs, calling and shouting as they approached the house.

---

[23] Pea soup.

They were not particularly friends, but they observed the French Canadian custom of visiting. Made hilarious by rounds of drinks, they stomped in, each kissing Grandmother, who tried to appear pleased with the visit and the familiarity, but she winced. Taking advantage of the liberty of the occasion, some of the men made salacious remarks. Drinks were passed and the men sang traditional songs. Some New Year's Eves several groups called on us. I cannot now understand why so many revelers came to our house—which was so far from town—when it was so cold. But they came. I was sorry for Grandmother, for I knew the condition and conduct of some of the men nauseated her.

On New Year's Day morning, Grandmother rose earlier than on other days. She was not rested, but she was happy. So was I. Today was her birthday. I stayed with her to help.

The men did the barn chores. During the forenoon some of the women guests came to help.

The boxstove was filled; its sides and top reddened. The parlor door was opened and the trap door at the top of the stairs was raised and fastened. I fed the farmer stove to keep the oven hot. Grandmother gave her last artistic touches to the roasts and turkeys. The roasting meat sizzled and the aroma filled the rooms.

The sleigh bells jingled over the hill. Down the snow-plowed roads the horses hurried to the sheltering shed. The joyous guests rushed in, tramping their feet at the door, slapping each other's backs, filling the house with merriment. When I was old enough to be trusted to care for the horses, it was my duty to unhitch them from the cutters and the sleighs, drive them to the barn, unharness them, blanket them, and tend to their feeding and care. I always considered this an imposition, as I hated leaving the festivities.

As each group of guests arrived, they laid their coats, scarves, bonnets, or caps on Grandmother's bed. They hurried to the stoves to warm their hands, commenting about the cold and the fragrance of the cooking food.

The older women went into the kitchen to help prepare dinner and garnish the table. The young people gathered in the parlor, exchanging jokes, reminiscing about the dance at last year's party. The older men sitting around the boxstove talked about work in the mines and the progress in the logging camps and shanties.

As noon approached, tables were set up end to end in the kitchen and spread with the ironed red tablecloth. The gilt-edged plates and cups and saucers clattered as they were set around the table. Chunks of golden butter and plates heaped with homemade bread were evenly spaced across the tables. On the smaller table sat, tantalizingly, frosted, decked cakes and re-warmed pies. On the open oven oval platters groaned with juicy, garlicky pork, dismembered and sliced turkeys, savory dressing, and rich, brown giblet gravy.

Dinner was called, and the adults converged on the kitchen.

The carafe was passed and toasts made to the New Year and Grandmother's birthday. There was merriment and singing. The children stood in the door, peering at the revelers. Later the children, Grandmother, and I ate together.

After the feast, a few women, Grandmother, and I did the kitchen work while the guests and other members of our household resumed their merrymaking. The older men sang French Canadian folk songs. In the parlor, the young folk gathered to sing to the accompaniment of the organ or played games like the exciting Post Office. After the tables were cleared and the work in the kitchen finished, some of the men took over the tables and settled in to play the card game Pedro.

The guests quieted with the fading afternoon. Supper was leftovers and hot tea. In the kitchen, we pushed the tables tightly along the walls and cleared the floor for the quadrille. The fiddle screeched and scraped as bodies swung to the shouts of the caller. The watchers stamped their feet and clapped their hands at the gusto of the darting dancers.

The evening hours passed and the revelers turned their attention to the lateness of the hour tick-tocking on the brass-faced clock.

Finally, the guests departed, and the jingle of the sleigh bells faded. The snow glistened to the smiling moon. The northern lights flashed high above the Huron Mountains.

Boreas[24] whistled gently. *Lou garou* howled. Early in the evening, some of the men and the teams had departed for the lumber camps in the woods: spring thaws would not wait—the logs could be hauled only over the smooth ice roads. Grandfather pressed the doors tight and latched them. Grandmother drew the curtains to ease the cold in the windows. The fire in the boxstove had dwindled to small embers, and the rooms were cooling fast.

Grandmother and I said the Rosary, then kissed.

"Bon soir, Grand'mere."

---

[24] The god of the North Wind.

Tilling the Soil

Life on a farm in the Upper Peninsula of Michigan in the late 1800s was finely tuned to the rhythms of nature. Spring brought warming soil and planting. Summer meant blueberries and sheep shearing, fall was a time of harvesting and butchering. Winter in this cold, northern state was the longest season of all, when most chores were done in the dark and the men disappeared to earn money cutting the huge white pine trees. And throughout all the seasons there was water to haul, wood to cut, wool to card, and a hundred other tasks necessary to feed and clothe a family. A boy growing up on that farm would understand these rhythms and become intimate with the land around him.

Hard Rocks and Furrow Lines

S eed was sown and underground vegetables were always planted when the moon was full or approaching fullness. The work could not be done when the moon was shrinking. If the moon was not full, it was absolutely necessary that the cycles of the moon point up.[25] If the cycle turned down, it was fatal to anything we did. The moon did not have to be visible, but it was diligently watched the night or day before the job was to be done.

Our tilled land had once been surrounded by primeval forest, consisting mainly of maple, birch, and big white pine; however, with the exception of a small grove around the house, all that forest had been cut, and an abundance of small trees had taken over. This second growth consisted mostly of poplar, balsam, white birch, hazel bushes, and soft maple saplings. The more level portions of our land had been cleared before I can recall, but before I left home in 1904, I helped clear the trees from the acreage on the broad slope facing the Huron Mountains.

Clearing the land was an off-season job—a between-busy-times job. After the seed was sown and planting finished in the spring, my grandfather selected a small patch of woods to clear in

---

[25] The horns, or pointed ends, of a crescent moon should point up.

order to expand the available land for planting. He cut out the trees and hauled the trimmed poles to the house for fuel. On Saturdays, he and I cleared stumps with one of the horse teams. We piled unwanted branches, stumps, and poles to dry, then burned them. As soon as we could, we broadcast rutabaga seed on the rough, unplowed ground and raked it in.[26]

After the land was clear of all the stumps and roots, our principal concern was directed to removing rocks. It was that drudging work, which we had to do every spring, that I disliked so much. After each plowing, there were as many rocks to remove as the previous year.

The soil of our farm was shallow, not more than two feet thick, and over a solid mass of volcanic rock. Plowing that soil was slow and exhausting work. The rocks were thick, the furrows irregular, and the surface of the ground was jagged. The stout walking-plow pulled by a team of draft horses struck the rocks and jarred my hands and arms so badly that I had to hold the handles at arms' length. When the plow struck a rock, it skidded out of the ground and slid over the surface. It had to be pulled back, the point redirected into the furrow, and then guided to the next rock.

We had to lift the loose rocks out of the furrows—very hard work—but many of the rocks were too large to lift, so we left them in place, and each year they gave us trouble.

---

[26] After seeds are planted, the earth is raked over them; the depth the seeds are raked into the ground depends on the type of seed.

After the ground was plowed, we had to pick the rocks two times—before and after the dragging.[27] As a boy, I did not do much plowing in the newly cleared ground. Manipulating a walking-plow was too heavy work for me, though I was put to dragging and picking rocks as soon as I was able to drive a team.

To gather rocks, we used a stoneboat[28] that was pulled by a draft team. The first stoneboat that I remember was a low, hand-made wooden sled. Because of the friction, the iron-bottomed stoneboat was hard to pull, though it slid easily over the snow in winter when we hauled barrels of water and stove wood. My grandfather invented another type: it was made of a large iron sheet taken from the tipple[29] of an abandoned iron ore mine and then bolted to the runners of a wooden sled.

Sometimes the rocks were too large to be hauled on a stone-boat, so we dragged them with a chain. We hauled them to fences, piled them around boulders in the fields, or rolled them into mine pits, of which there were several nearby. When we cleared land near the Escanaba River, we pushed some into the stream.

---

[27] This was probably done with a drag harrow, a device pulled by a horse and consisting of long spikes arranged in rows. It was used both to break up dirt clumps and flatten the earth for planting and to rake in the seeds after they were sown.

[28] A type of sleigh whose carrier is not supported by runners like a sled, but, rather, sits flat on the ground.

[29] A place where cars carrying mined ore from underground are tipped and emptied of their contents.

Except for a few bushels of *pois* that we sold, we consumed our crops ourselves. The oats—the largest crop—were mainly for the horses. Barley was for the pigs, and a few bushels of wheat and rye fed the poultry. In later years, some of the wheat was milled into brown flour for our home.

My grandfather was certain that seed broadcast by hand grew better than that sowed by mechanical seeders, about which we had heard much and seen pictures of in catalogues. I began to help my grandfather sow grain at a very early age and when I see the painting "The Sower" by Jean-François Millet,[30] I am reminded of those days.

On the day of sowing, we hauled sacks of seed on the stone-boat and dropped them at convenient places around the field. Grandfather paced off the distance that he could cast the seed with his hand and then placed several little white flags in a line. With a sack of seed hung from his right shoulder and resting against his left side, he strode down the line of flags.

With his left hand holding the sack open he rhythmically sent his right hand into the sack and, with a sweep of the arm, sent the seed scattering. At each stride, he swept his hand. Down the line of flags he went as I followed and moved the flags a specific number

---

[30] According to the website of the Carnegie Museum of Art, which owns one of Millet's "The Sower" paintings, "'The Sower' is Millet's most famous theme and one he repeated several times between 1850 and 1870."

of steps to the right, or to the left. Up the field he went until we reached the fence or the underbrush. He refilled from one of the bags in the field, then we started back. So up and down the field we went until the whole field was sown.

Jean-François Millet's "The Sower."

Immediately after the seed was broadcast, the soil was ready for dragging. The teeth of the drag were set[31] for the particular type of seed. This was a job I could do well; sometimes I dragged until dark. In the partially cleared, irregularly shaped areas that were still stumpy, Grandfather broadcast the seed by walking among the stumps and scattering the seed with broken sweeps of his arms. Then the ground was hand-raked instead of being dragged.

Each spring, a small patch of ground was cleared of brush and then burnt over. We lacerated the surface of that ground with iron hand rakes, then broadcast rutabaga or turnip seeds. To avoid burying the seed too deeply, we pulled a small balsam bough over the surface rather than dragging or raking it.

Year after year the fields expanded, finally compelling us to purchase mechanical seed broadcasters. The first one had a canvas sack that was suspended by a strap over the sower's neck and rested against the breast. The sack contained about two pecks of seed and the broadcasting mechanism was operated by a rapidly turned hand crank. The seed flowed out of the sack through an adjustable opening at the bottom where it fell onto a revolving disk that scattered the seed. Grandfather had to turn the crank and walk in a coordinated way to broadcast the seed evenly.

---

[31] Metal tines protruded beneath the machine and could be extended if more earth was needed to cover the seed or retracted if less was needed.

The second seeder we purchased was similar to the first, except that the broadcasting mechanism was cuplike and the seed whirled out at a right angle to the sower's body. That was the most modern seeder we ever owned.

Diligently and anxiously, we watched our crops grow and ripen. The rusted scythes were taken from the wooden pegs poking from the walls of the buggy shed and honed to a razor's edge on the big, turning grindstone. Grinding the scythes was an after-supper job that I disliked very much. Turning the grindstone was not arduous, but it was monotonous, and sometimes we worked late into the night in the dim light of a kerosene lamp that attracted pesky mosquitoes. After each scythe blade was sharpened, it was fitted to a curved handle.

Each day, as the grain ripened and yellowed, Grandfather inspected it. He took samples from the yellowest heads, rolled them between his hands to loosen the kernels, and chewed pinches of kernels to test their firmness.

One evening, he told us that in the morning the harvesting would begin. Besides Grandfather and my two uncles, we usually had at least one hired man to do the mowing. Each man examined his scythe and a handstone,[32] adjusted the handgrips[33] to his swing

---

[32] Sharpening stone.
[33] The long, curved blade of the scythe was attached to a long handle. From this handle protruded two short wooden grips, which were used to hold the tool.

and stride, and tried a few practice swaths at the edge of the field. Early the next morning before the dew evaporated, the mowing began. In the field, one man took the lead, going to the left.

Measuring the full sweep of his scythe, he began at the rocks in the fence. Down the perimeter of the field he went, followed by the other men. Swish, swish, rhythmically and with an even pace they advanced, sweeping the scythes the full lengths of their arms, cutting even strips as they went. When they arrived at the end of the field, they advanced clockwise. On and on they mowed, around and around the field, stopping only for drinks from a water pail that I or one of the women had carried to the edge of the field. At intervals, they stopped to sharpen the scythes—resting the tips of the handles on the ground and sharpening the blades with hand-stones.

Some of the seed had been cast among the stone fences and had grown into fine grain, so after the men had mowed the field, one of them nipped the stray stalks along the fences and around the rock piles with a hand sickle, throwing the stalks on the field to be raked.

As soon as the fallen grain stalks—along with the grass and the weeds that had been cut with them—were sufficiently dry, the tangled lot was raked with wooden hand rakes and immediately piled into cocks[34] to cure. If rain soaked the cocks, they were opened and scattered to dry, then re-raked, re-cocked, and hauled.

One summer day, someone brought a cradle scythe,[35] a more modern and efficient reaping tool than the simple scythe. When the men cut the grain with simple scythes, the cut stalks lay thinly on the ground and had to be raked by hand, which scattered the grain—a lot was lost. We had tried a horse-drawn rake, but horses' tramping hooves and the way the rake's teeth rolled and scattered the grain caused even greater loss. In contrast, the cradle scythe put the stalks in neat and even piles. Those little piles could be gathered into larger piles and bound into sheaves. The cradle scythe was a great improvement.

Gathering the little heaps the cradle scythe created was slow and, although light work, fatiguing. Each day's reaping was planned so that when we finished the day's work, all the grain that had been cut was sheaved and shocked.[36] To make the sheaves, the little piles made by the cradle scythes were gathered into piles large enough for sheaves and bound with bands we made by twisting straw.

---

[34] Small, cone-shaped piles of hay left in the field to dry.
[35] A cradle scythe has four long, parallel cutting blades instead of the single blade of a simple scythe.
[36] A shock is a bundle of sheaves set on end with the cut part of the stalk down.

A method of binding sheaves was introduced on our farm that I have not seen on any other farm. I do not know where the idea originated, but one summer we began to use hazel wattles[37] I cut from the nearby woods instead of straw. Sheaves bound with wattles could be much larger than those bound with straw bands.

In about 1900, we bought a secondhand table reaper.[38] Although it appeared to be a very old machine, it was a great improvement over our usual method of cutting with scythes. A quarter-circle platform was attached to the back of the cutting bar on which the grain fell as it was cut, then a device with four rakes—each the length of the cutting bar—would rotate and pile the grain at the edge of the platform. When the pile grew large enough to make a sheaf, the driver pushed a foot lever to lower the rakes, and the pile was pushed off the platform. The pile was then ready for sheaving.

The modern binder[39] did not come into our neighborhood until about 1902 when we bought a McCormick binder. We had the only binder in the area of Champion, Michigamme, Republic, and Humbolt.

---

[37] Probably thin branches.

[38] A reaper is a grain-cutting mechanical device pulled behind horses; it is much more efficient than scythes.

[39] A machine for binding the sheaves.

The grain stalks were stored in mows[40] and in the barn loft to await threshing.[41] Our first thresher was a small, one-horse tread-powered machine. A crew of four men operated it. One man forked the stalks of grain from the mow to a small platform where a feeder spread the grain and pushed it into a cylinder. At the rear of the separator, another man removed the straw and sacked the grain as it came out of a shaking spout. The fourth man drove the horse on the tread-power and helped at other jobs as needed. When I became old enough, I assumed the job of watching the horse on the tread-power.

Our second threshing outfit was much bigger but also horse powered. The separator was large enough to make it profitable for us to rent it and our labor to surrounding farms, so we did the threshing for miles around. The last separator was run by horse-sweep power; that is, the horses were hitched to the end of sweeps (long poles) that turned the machinery. Four teams furnished the power as they pulled round and round in a circle. The driver of the teams sat on a platform resting over the middle of the power.

We never used the threshing machine on our *pois*; they were always flailed,[42] because the cylinder of the threshing machine split the peas. No split peas for French Canadian *soupe de pois*!

---

[40] Piles of grain stalks.

[41] The process of separating the grain from the stalks.

[42] Separating the peas from their pods with a flail, which looks like a long stick with a short stick loosely attached to the top. The flailer

We probably had no more than one big load of peas to flail each harvest. During odd times, whoever did the chores in the barn, spread some pea vines on the floor between the two mows and slammed the flail as he stepped around the pile.

The loosened peas dropped to the floor and when the flailer thought the peas were all depodded, he pitched their vines in the mow. The *pois* were then swept into a small pile and scooped into a winnower.

The winnower was a semi-circular, flat-bottomed platform with a handle on each side. A person lifted the winnower to his waist and jerked it up and down, forward and backward, until the peas were in the bottom and separated from the bits of vines, chaff, and other dirt.[43] With a large wooden comb, he cleared away the waste and then poured the peas into a basket.

If the *pois* cooked well, Grandmother made *soupe de pois*. If not, they were fed to the pigs.

---

holds the long stick and whacks the stalks with the short stick, popping the peas off the stalks.

[43] This process is depicted in Jean-François Millet's painting "The Winnower," of which Millet painted several versions.

Jean-François Millet's "The Winnower."

Scorching Pigs

Pigs were always butchered on a clear, crisp day in late fall. It had to be done during certain signs of the moon. The fuller the moon, the better the result. If hogs or cows were butchered when the moon was not full, the meat would be rancid and tough, and shrink even in the coldest weather. However, the moon did not need to be shining nor the work done at night.

A few days before a pig was to be butchered, it was impounded alone in a dry, sheltered pen with plenty of dry straw to lie on.

Big, round-bottomed kettles for heating water were hung from poles over the stone fireplace across the road from the house and filled with water hauled in barrels on a jumper from Dalliba pit. From the mow, dry straw was hauled on the wagon rack to the fireplace. Several stones were placed on the ground in two parallel rows to hold the pig on its back after it was dead. A scaffold built in a tree to hoist the pig was inspected. The knives were ground sharp, and the hoes were handy for the scraping.

The squealing, barley-fattened pig was driven to a corner in the fence. A hind leg was jerked back and a rope tied to it. Grandfather grabbed its ear and yanked it to its side. Someone stepped on its hind leg to clamp it to the ground while someone else straightened a foreleg and knelt on it. The other foreleg was held up. A rope was looped to the pig's upper jaw and the head pulled back tight. The pig squealed and grunted. A place under its neck was shaved and washed. Standing by during the preparation for killing the pig distressed me. It seemed that the procedure took so long that the pig suffered in the waiting.

Grandfather ran his thumb along the blade of the stabbing-knife to test the sharpness of the edge. He placed his knee on the pig's head and looked at Grandmother, who stood near with an iron skillet. The pig winced, strained, and stiffened as the long blade entered its neck. Grandmother squatted in front of the pig, pressed the edge of the skillet under the incision in the neck, and, with one hand, churned the blood—later she would make delicious, garlicky blood sausage. The pig strained, its legs stiffened, and its eyes began to close. It relaxed and gasped. Another dead pig.

The men carried the pig by its legs and placed it on its back between the row of rocks, its rump to the wind. They covered its body with dry straw, and with a handful of long torches made of burning straw, set the straw-covered pig afire. After the hair and bristles burned, the men scraped the scorched parts with the hoes and big knives. Then the pig was turned and burned and scraped until it was clean.

They placed the pig on a large table and, with hot water from the kettles, thoroughly scraped and washed away the black dirt and ashes. The thin parts of the ears and the slim portion of the tail were crisply roasted, cut off, and eaten at once as a part of the ritual of butchering. If any of the skin on the body was scorched, it also was good. The tips of the burnt hair and bristles stayed in the rind to give the pork a particularly distinct and pleasant flavor.

The pig was then hung by the hind legs and dressed.[44]

The pig's bladder was inflated to its utmost, dried, and a portion of the open end removed—it had been turned into a tobacco pouch. Sometimes I was favored with being permitted to keep the bladder so that, while it was inflated, I used it as a football.

---

[44] Cut open and internal organs removed.

Maple Syrup

My memory lingers on the few aged maple trees that grew near the house, their robust, dark-gray bark interlaced with fine green moss. I remember, as March approached, the crusted, thawing snow, the warbling, twittering, nesting birds among the tangled branches, and the sweet, and sparkling drops of sap with their promise of the unmatchable flavor of maple syrup.

When the snow melted during the day but froze at night, making a hard crust, we began to ready our equipment and to watch for signs that the sap was rising in the maples. Our equipment was primitive. The sap-catchers were of three kinds—small tin pails, hewed-out wooden troughs, and birch-bark troughs. The sap catchers were stored in the shed so they were handy for scouring and cleaning. When it came time to use them, they had become dusty, and some needed to be repaired or replaced.

As the sap rose, the bark of the maples began to dampen and the snow at the roots of the maples melted, leaving bowl-like holes at the bases. Grandmother asked me to carry the catchers into the kitchen where she could examine them. The spouts were made of cedar wood. If the wood had split, the spouts were discarded. We had seen pictures of metal spouts in catalogs; but we never had any.

When I was young, Grandfather made the spouts, but after I was old enough to help Grandmother with the maple-making chores, it became my job to make the spouts in the workshop, which was in an old log house nearby. I selected a piece of well-seasoned and straight-grained cedar about a foot long and split it into square sticks a little larger than a spout. Then with my jack-knife or a drawknife,[45] I whittled it into a round stick. Two inches or so from one end I whittled away half of the rounded stick then grooved the remaining part. With a bit, I bored a hole lengthways in the long part of the stick. That was the portion of the spout that was driven into the tree.

One school day, Grandmother would call my attention to the wet bark, and the next Saturday, we tapped the maples (unless a snow storm interfered). As soon as the chores were finished on that Saturday, we hurried into the grove and Grandmother pointed out the maples whose sap was running most. With an inch bit and a brace, I bored a hole about waist high into a trunk, then pounded a spout into the hole. In that manner, I went from maple to maple.

The pails were hung from the spouts; but the cans and troughs were adjusted on the bare roots or trampled snow. If snow fell in

---

[45] A blade with a handle at each end. The blade is pulled—or drawn—toward the user.

the cans and troughs during the night, I had to scoop them out before going to school. If the snow melted during the day, the troughs sometimes turned on their sides, spilling the sap.

During the syrup-making days, I had to gather the sap while there was still daylight. I went from maple to maple with two buckets hung from a yoke over my shoulders. The crust on the snow sometimes softened so much during the day that I awkwardly broke through, spilling the sap. I poured what I had collected into one or two barrels in a corner of the kitchen until there was enough to boil in the round-bottomed iron kettles.

We put about a half barrel of sap in a kettle hung from a cross pole at a place far enough from the house to prevent the heat from damaging the trees. As soon as the morning was light enough, I went to the kettles, shoveled and swept away the snow that had accumulated about them, and started a fire with dry wood from the shed. While the fire was making headway, I carried buckets full of sap from the barrels in the kitchen. I carefully watched the warming sap and when it was about to reach the boiling point, I reduced the fire so that the sap evaporated but did not boil, because boiling affected the flavor. As the sap evaporated and lowered in the kettles, I replenished it.

While she was at work in the kitchen, Grandmother kept careful watch on the kettles. When she thought that the sap must be turning into syrup, she went out and, with a long-handled ladle, dipped from the kettle and tasted. I watched her with delight, for when she lifted her eyebrows, smiled, and smacked her lips, it was time to transfer the thickened sap to the boiler on the hot farmer stove in the kitchen. There, Grandmother took over to finish making the syrup. When evening arrived, there were probably two quarts of syrup in the boiler. The syrup was then poured into glass jars or a jug. A lot of work for so little maple syrup—but it was so good.

We did not make more than six or seven gallons of maple syrup in one season, and I do not recall ever having sold any. When the snow had almost entirely disappeared and the trees were budding, the sap lost its delicate flavor. We gathered our equipment, cleaned it carefully, and stored it to await the next spring.

After the spring season had so far advanced that the doors could be left open and we could sit outside, Grandmother invited a few friends and relatives to a maple syrup party on a Sunday. Because it was too early in the spring for us to have many eggs, each family was required to bring a contribution of eggs. When the time to eat arrived, Grandmother boiled syrup in a broad, shallow pan and the women poached eggs in it. We ate all we desired. Anyone who did not care for poached eggs could have bread to dunk in a bowl of maple syrup.

It was a great treat for our guests, and they looked forward to the gathering with delight. I have never heard of any other people who enjoyed maple syrup more nor ate it in the manner that we French Canadians did.

About Sheep

T ending our sheep and working with the wool was one duty that delighted Grandmother. Our small flock provided us with mutton to eat and some cash when the mutton was sold at the country store in Champion. All the wool was made into articles of apparel by the women of the household. Grandmother enjoyed every step in the process, from the lambs dropping in the spring to the finished product. She and I were close companions in all of that work.

Sheep were not only the small farmer's friend, they were the backwoods farmer's most essential friend. So it was with us on that rocky coteau[46] farm: our sheep provided a substantial part of our necessities.

On small farms, especially those with wood lots and areas too rolling for cultivation, sheep are useful land-clearers, consuming many plants that browsing animals won't touch—thistle shoots, goldenrod, sourgrass, sunflower leaves, raspberry bushes, tender twigs, and leaves. And when those feeds are exhausted, they'll munch on briary blackberry vines and roots. They are very persistent in their craving for salt. I have seen sheep eat stumps, roots of

---

[46] A hilly upland.

trees, and even the ground to get salt. Many times, I have watched them lick salty stones until the surfaces were shiny. Yet, they require little water. In winter, when water is scarce, they do very well licking snow. Give sheep free access to salt, plenty of coarse grass, twigs in the paddocks, and dirty hay and straw in the barn-yard (often mixed with manure), and they thrive.

Our sheep were our pets and usually numbered a few more than twenty—two bucks and the remainder ewes. Sheep require shelter only from the blasting, cold wind, and the only confinement we gave ours was a little sheepfold in one dark corner of the cattle barn as protection from the howling wind and prowling dogs (wolves never bothered them). The barn was a pioneer's structure built of chinked and plastered logs and with a sagging roof. But the place was comfortable.

Barn and other buildings on the farm.

It always seemed strange to me how those sheep could be butted about by the horned cattle without serious injury. Sheep do not just look sheepish, they are sheepish, and they are the most patient and forgiving animals, unless the other animals are dogs.

Sometimes a buck will develop the habit of butting[47] with its head, which becomes quite annoying. Regardless of how dumb a ram is, it always knows from what direction to charge a person— from behind. And they are persistent. Once a butting young buck becomes a ram he continues to be a butting ram. Hit such a ram across the nose with a stick and he will shake his head and sniffle, and maybe rub his nose against the ground, his front hoofs, or his shanks; but while he is relieving his pain, he will stare upward at his tormentor as if to say, "I'll get even with you!"

As soon as the ground began to freeze and the blizzardy snow to annoy them too much, the sheep crowded more compactly together to graze in flock formation, advancing, moving with the wind, always edging nearer and nearer to the south side of the barn, and pressing their way among the wheels, wagons, racks, tools, and farm implements in the open-front shed. They ate straw from a large pile in the barnyard, fraying big holes to lie in. But we had to be watchful to prevent them from digging too deeply into the stack and causing it to collapse. One winter, several of our sheep were

---

[47] Wilfred repeatedly uses the word "bunting" instead of "butting," which gives the impression of "bunting" as a regional usage.

smothered under a pile of straw. As the sheep helped themselves to the straw, they circled around the pile until they were hidden from the blizzard; but they also got an occasional taste of nice hay that had been trampled into the ground by the colt, the old mare, and the few cows. I also sometimes gave them a handful of oats or barley, or a snack of salt. No crowding please!

We did not clean the sheepfold every day, so the black droppings of manure and the litter were allowed to accumulate. Straw was dumped over the partition for the sheep to eat, then they would hoof the remainder for bedding. The mixture grew into a thick mat that was laboriously removed every few days and that was my job on Saturdays. Cleaning meant the sheep had to lie on the cold, damp, hard floor. They would indulge in short lay-downs, then get up and look for soft dry spots—hoofing at the planks as they did so. So, as winter progressed, the wool on their rumps and under-bellies became dark gray mats.

Ewes dropped their lambs in late March and early April. We watched the ewes carefully as the time approached. When a ewe began to detach herself from the huddling flock and to hoof into the thick damp mat of manure, she was segregated and put in a small fold made from an empty, boarded-up stall. That prevented the other sheep from trampling, injuring, or sometimes killing the lambs.

Lambs are often twins—triplets are not uncommon—but quads cause excitement and are very welcome. During lambing season, it was necessary for someone to visit the expectant ewes several times each night to be present when the lambs were dropped in the private folds, and also to watch for unexpected births in the bigger folds so the lambs could at once be protected. If the nights were particularly cold, newborn lambs were wrapped in swaddling blankets and carried to the house where they were placed in a well-insulated box near the living room boxstove, which was kept warm during the lambing season. Nurse-maiding those lambs was part of my chores. After being up much of the night caring for lambs and ewes, I still had to tend to my regular early-morning chores. I took my young charges with me to the barn while I attended to the other stock. Hanging my lantern from a beam above the ewes, I held the young one near its ewe and pushed its mouth to the ewe's teats. The lamb at once began to suck and butt, while the ewe looked back fondly as the thick milk oozed from the little mouth and trickled down its chin and neck. After my barn chores were finished, I carried the lamb back to its comfortable little fold behind the boxstove where Grandmother tended to it the remainder of the day, or until I returned from school. When the weather was mild, Grandmother occasionally carried the lamb to the barn for nursing during the day.

Caring for the lambs in this way lasted four or five days. Since there were usually about thirty lambs, occasionally more than one lamb had to be nursed. Sometimes nature did not deal kindly with a ewe. If a ewe's milk was not good or sufficient, her hungry lambs stole from other ewes, and that was detrimental to the lambs of those ewes. When that happened, I had to carry the lamb to the house and feed it warmed cow's milk from a nipple bottle. I held the bottle for the lamb while it was in its little box in the kitchen. Long, wobbly ears flapping, eyes bulging, it staggered in circles to follow the bottle, bumping its black-button nose against the nipple. This was exciting and fun: the lambs thrived surprisingly well on cow's milk and became my staunch friends.

When a lamb had outgrown the little box-fold and it was able to endure the spring cold, we left it with the ewe. After that, like Mary's little lamb, it followed anyone with a milk bottle.

Usually, lambs suckle until they outgrow it or until the ewe's teats become dry and sore. It is very amusing to see a lamb nearly as large as its mother get down on its knees, hind end up and tail waving, while sucking. Sometimes a ewe got so much punishment from the butting nose of the lamb that she would draw up a leg and kick. Then the lamb looked about for another lunch counter; lambs are persistent little thieves. I do not recall ever having seen a ewe deliberately abandon her lamb, regardless of all the nose jabbing, as long as she had milk, though I have been told that ewes do sometimes desert their little ones like some humans do.

Sometimes if a ewe lost her baby by death she was given one for adoption, an orphan or one whose mother could not nurse it sufficiently. Ewes are kind, adoptive mothers, and sometimes they entice lambs to abandon their own mamas.

About Sheep

When the lambs were about four weeks old, they were permitted to accompany the ewes into the barn lot, even while the cattle were in the barn. Lambs are snoopy little creatures, and they have great curiosity for moving objects, such as the legs of cows and horses. I have seen them smacked hard—too hard it seemed for little lambs—but I never saw one killed or injured from being kicked.

Sometimes it was mid-June before the ground was warm enough for the lambs to be out at night. When enough snow had melted and the frost moderated so that grass and coarse vegetation were available, we let the sheep into one of the poorer paddocks for the summer. Of course, on a cold night we scurried to open the paddock gate by which a big blotch of sheep had already assembled so they could rush to the barn to seek shelter.

Sheep have delicate noses and keen eyes, stretching necks, tough skins, and long hooking tongues. They have a way of finding openings and weak places in fences. Ordinary wire, pole, and rail fences were not tight or strong enough to confine sheep. If a fence was constructed of ordinary single-strand barbed wire, the lowest strand had to be near the ground and it had to be very tight; because sheep are exceedingly persistent when they see and scent better forage outside their paddock. That the grass is greener on the other side of the fence is no meaningless saying to sheep!

The sheep knew when they had trespassed; when they saw me advancing in their direction after they had ventured into a forbidden field, they lowered their heads guiltily and sneaked farther from the gate or hurried back to re-enter their paddocks. But as soon as I was over the hill from them, they began to sneak toward the damaged fence. When autumn arrived, bunched wool in almost continuous lines was impaled on the barbs; sometimes there was so much that Grandmother and I found gathering it worthwhile.

After the lambs had passed the frisking age they were docked —their tails hacked off to leave a stub about two inches long. It was necessary to shorten their tails, because otherwise all kinds of dirt, cockles, thistle burs, briars, and dry leaf stems caught in them. If the tails were not removed before the summer had progressed far, they became sore and the lambs' growth was affected.

The men docked the lambs' tails by either of two methods, neither of which was refined, scientific, or humane. In one method, a rusty, poorly sharpened pocket knife was used: its tormentor severed the tail at a joint and then "cauterized" the raw end with a handful of salt, though sometimes it was not cauterized at all. Ouch! The other method was to place the tail on a block of wood and hack it off with an axe. The lamb then ran off flipping the stub, scampering to the huddled flock to lick its wounds and look back as though pleading for sympathy.

After the lambs had been weaned and the young bucks were large enough to be slaughtered, we sold all but one or two to the local butcher. How I suffered seeing those lambs, their legs bound like sticks, dumped into the wagon's box and left broiling in the blazing sun, waiting to be transported to town!

The bucks that we kept back were used for breeding. We always selected the best young ewes to propagate the flock, but ours was a badly inbred flock: there were no other bucks in the adjacent country and I cannot recall one having been brought to our farm for breeding. We did not know anything about heredity.

When the weather became consistently warm, the sheep had to be sheared, but shearing had to be done at the right time to get the best quality wool. We sheared them as soon as the nightly frosts had ceased and the wool was beginning to shed. If it was done too early in the spring, the sheep suffered from the cold. They bunched in sheltered places, crowding out the lambs, who could not jam themselves in. If a lamb did get in, it might be injured or crushed to death. Sheep are so helpless and dependent that they arouse sympathy, and it was distressful to see them trying to protect themselves in a cold wind.

But, if shearing was put off too long and too much of the wool was shed, large bunches of it snagged on twigs, branches, small stumps, weeds, and the barbed wire fences. Also, the men would have to clip away new growth where it had become entangled with the old growth.

Shearing sheep was a disagreeable job for non-expert hands—and none of our folks were experts. The whole procedure was a bungled job that was very distressing to the sheep. Usually the shearing was done by the men of the household. Occasionally, a hired man helped, but the men of the family had some sympathy toward the sheep that the hired hands did not.

The day before the shearing, the shears were sharpened on the big disk grindstone that I turned with a crank, then honed with a little whetstone to make the blades razor-sharp and the points fine.

We had two kinds of shears: ordinary, large scissors used for cutting cloth and regular wool clippers with two long triangular blades joined at one end by a flat steel semicircular spring. Because we owned just one pair of clippers, we had to use scissors as well.

Early on the day of the shearing, the flock was driven into the small maple grove by the house or into a temporary paddock in one corner of the barnyard. Although they are supposed to be stupid, the sheep seemed to have a premonition of what was going to happen; they huddled together and crowded into a corner in the fence, looking over their shoulders, wiggling their noses, and blinking.

A long bench from the farm workshop and the mess table from the kitchen were placed under the maples. To get one of the sheep, the shearer strode to the huddled mob, grabbed a sheep by its ear, and either dragged or lifted it by the scruff of the neck and the rump. Cruelly, it was thumped on the bench and held on its back until it lay still. If a sheep was particularly obstreperous its rump was slammed on the ground and it was held viselike between the shearer's legs.

About Sheep

The most efficient procedure for shearing a sheep was to place the animal on its back, legs sticking up, and then begin at the ewe's udders or the buck's scrotum. The wool was shorter and thinner along the belly and therefore not so badly matted and tangled as along the sides and the back. The first thing the shearer did was to cut a straight opening in the wool along the middle of the belly. That apparently was very painful because the helpless sheep flinched, jerked, and twitched. Sometimes an I-don't-care shearer would cut pieces of skin and flesh. "As meek as a lamb" is not a meaningless expression.

After the line of insertion into the belly wool was made, the sheep was rolled onto its side and little narrow strips were clipped from rear to front and up along the neck to the jaws. Then the clipping progressed along the sides and legs and on one side of the neck. When that side was done, the sheep was rolled over and the procedure repeated.

When the shearing was done, the sheep kicked itself to the ground and stumbled back to the flock where it wedged itself in and licked its wounds. The other sheep seemed to look at it with abhorrence, sympathy, and apprehension.

A sheep, especially an old ewe that has just been sheared, is a very ugly animal. Its rounded graceful form has suddenly been divested of its padding, and there it stands with a long, wrinkled neck that swings a hammer-like head; long, flopping ears; crooked, spindly legs with knotty joints; and a bulging belly.

The wool clips were immediately carried into the buggy shed and hung over poles to dry until the women could wash them. The tightly matted wool was almost like a pile of dried dung, so cleaning it was a tedious and disagreeable job. But it had to be well cleaned to satisfy Grandmother's exacting requirements.

The wool was washed out-of-doors in front of the tool shed. Grandmother was boss, and she inspected each stage of the cleaning. On wool-washing days, about three barrels of rainwater were grouped near the big iron kettles, each of which contained nearly one barrel of water. Those were the general-purpose kettles in which we cooked barley, peas, and other grains for hog feed, and in which we also reduced our maple sap to syrup.

The women used only clear water without soap to wash the wool. When the water was warm enough, a clip of wool was carried from the shed and dropped into the kettle where it soaked and simmered as it was stirred to loosen the dirt and dissolve the manure and clabber.[48] The stinky mess was poked, swirled, and pulled apart, after which it was lifted with a stick and transferred to a kettle with cleaner water.

After the dung was dissolved to the consistency of mud and the straw, twigs, and other debris extracted, the wool was rinsed several times in lukewarm water in wooden tubs. Next the wool

---

[48] Wilfred uses clabber to refer specifically to cow manure.

was boiled, then lifted from the second kettle to another and back again until the last bit of syrupy substance had been removed.

Finally the women wrung and twisted the wool by hand, then hung it on clothes lines to dry in the sun. The slightly stirring air loosened and fluffed the wool. The wool was then carefully piled on the rug in the parlor for the night. The next day, it was once again hung in the sun, after which it was wrapped in large canvas cloth or poked into burlap sacks. It was inspected several times during the warm weather to prevent roaches, bugs, and weevils from damaging it. When cold weather set in, some of the wool would be sold and the remainder made into articles for the household.

From then on, during odd moments or in the evenings after the general household duties were finished, the women carried armfuls of wool into the kitchen or, before dark in the fall, out to the maple trees. There they leisurely pulled and pinched the wool, extracting every particle of straw, leaves, twigs, and other coarse matter. The fluffy heaps of wool were carefully deposited in a pile on a clean sheet or on newspapers spread on the floor in a well-guarded corner—we had to watch for bugs—until Grandmother was ready to card and spin and knit it into clothes.

A Winter Day on the Farm

When frost struck hard in late August, the men took the teams to work in the logging camps in the Huron Mountains and in the pulpwood shanties[49] down the Escanaba River and toward Channing, Powers, and other little towns, leaving Grandmother and me, and my two aunts until they married, to tend to the chores that the men had done in the barn and around the farm. We were kept busy during the short winter days.

My day began when Grandmother called to me from her bed. If I did not stir, she tapped a broom handle against the ceiling until my feet thumped the floor. I did my best to avoid causing her such trouble.

If Grandmother had not gotten up in the night to refuel the boxstove, the house was as cold as the outdoors. Rushing to the trapdoor at the top of the stairs, I descended feet first and hurried to dress in the clothes and shoes, or large rubbers or shoepacks,[50] I

---

[49] Lumber-company-run bunkhouses, dining halls, and other buildings inhabited by lumbermen who cut softwoods for making pulp, which is turned into paper.

[50] Shoepacks were a popular Finnish article of footwear worn by hunters, workers in the woods, and school boys. High-topped and

had laid out near the stove the night before. If the house was cold, I started a fire using cedar shavings I had made with my jackknife the previous night, then donned my heavy mackinaw,[51] scarf, and fur cap and ran outdoors to struggle my way through the snowdrifts to the barn.

From her bed, Grandmother watched the boxstove to see that its sides and top did not become too hot. When any part of the boxstove or the iron stovepipe reddened, she got up, shut off the draft, and returned to bed. After the room was warm, she went to the kitchen and lit the fire in the farmer stove.

If the weather was not very cold, the barn steamed from the cow clabber, horse manure, and sheep droppings. On the coldest mornings all the animal excreta was frozen stiff and brown icicles hung from the beams. If there was any milking to do, which was unusual at that time of winter, I did the milking first. The cows were not groomed after squishing in their clabber, and conditions were not very sanitary, but I never knew of anyone who complained about the unnatural color of the milk or any bad taste.

When the temperature was very cold, the barn was not much warmer than outside. I shoveled the yellowish balls of horse manure and the slabs of cow clabber through the two small, square

shaped somewhat like a Dutch wooden shoe combined with a moccasin, they were soft, comfortable, and warm. Their only drawback was the pliability of the soles, which made footing uncertain on the snow.
[51] A short, double-breasted coat of heavy wool.

openings in the wall, the bottoms of which were about shoulder high. Cleaning the barn and the stable was not much of a job until the tops of the manure piles outside were above the doors, then the manure had to be handled twice: first shoveled out, then forked farther away. Since the manure piles were on the north side of the barn, that job was unpleasant, as the wind-swirled manure dust and straw penetrated my clothes and swished in my face.

After the barn was cleaned, I fed the animals. The hay was in the loft above the stock and the straw was in a mow in the shed that adjoined one end of the barn, which helped insulate against the cold and the wind. The hay was in a great mass and thoroughly tangled. I had to laboriously pull it apart, fork it over to a square hole in the ceiling, push it down, then distribute it to the cows that were to freshen[52] in the early spring. I forked straw to the other cattle and to the colts, horses, and sheep.

After finishing the barn chores, I returned to the house and made sure the two water pails at the end of the sink were full and, if it was wash day, the tubs and barrels also. I saw to it that there was a big rick of wood behind each stove—the farmer stove in the kitchen and the ravenous boxstove in the living room. Grandmother never reminded me of those chores, so if I did not keep diligent watch, she did the jobs herself. To neglect my duties and thereby cause her to do hard work unnecessarily deeply shamed me.

---

[52] Begin producing milk.

Water was constantly kept in a big copper boiler on the back of the farmer stove. Dipping the tin wash basin into the boiler, I got enough warm water to remove as much of the soilure[53] and dirt as possible. Sometimes Grandmother washed my neck and ears— painlessly. Breakfast nearly always consisted of fried salt pork and French pancakes or French toast. We always had tea, never coffee. After breakfast, I took my lunch pail and went to school.

In winter, school ended at 3:30 o'clock as dark was setting in. The way home was to the north, so, many times, I had to walk backwards because of the beating wind and the dry snow that cut my face and wrists and slashed into my clothes. By the time I arrived over the ridge and I could see the house, a little light beckoned from the kitchen window: Grandmother had washed the globe of my lantern and filled the base with kerosene so that I would waste no time getting to my chores.

Quickly changing to my stinky clothes, I hurried to the barn to let out the stock, singly or in groups, to drink. I have seen weather so bad that cattle would not leave the barn; they preferred remaining thirsty. I did lead the horses to the well, though sometimes they just stuck their noses in the water, shook their heads, turned their rumps to the wind, and humped their backs. No drink.

There were two wells near the barn; however, as winter wore on, they became very inadequate, freezing solid or draining

---

[53] A stain or spot.

dry. Those wells had been dug by drilling and blasting into solid rock. Each well was covered with a wooden box with a frame extending upward and from which hung a pulley with one sheave.[54] A small, stout wire chain passed over the sheave and buckets hung from each end of the chain. When one bucket reached the top of the well and was being emptied, the other bucket was dipping and filling.

The horses were watered first, because the cattle with their sharp horns could not be trusted. The sheep preferred snow to water, and, as they did not drink much, I would frequently just fill a couple of buckets with snow and dump it into their trough.

When the wells were frozen solid or dry, I either hauled water from Dalliba pit or drove the cattle there to drink. To get water from the pit, I put two barrels on a jumper to which I hitched the old mare. That required a great deal of hard work since I had to carry the water from the barrels in buckets to the cattle; none of the animals got enough water. On Saturdays I always drove the cattle over a trail that I first broke in the deep snow. At the pit, I chipped a couple of holes in the thick ice through which the cattle drank. Sometimes the snow and cold were so severe that when the cattle got to the top of the ridge, some of them left the trail and, circumventing me, ran back to the barn.

---

[54] A sheave is a grooved wheel. The chain or rope holding the bucket runs along the groove.

I pushed the cow clabber and horse manure that had dropped during the day back from under the animals and pulled armfuls of coarse weeds out of the mangers and strew them among the legs for bedding. Then I filled the mangers again with straw or hay, depending on the stock. The chickens and other fowl were roosting and all I had to do was turn some of them around so that their droppings did not fall on the cattle.

The last thing I did was inspect the halters and tethers to see that the horses were secure in their stalls and that the cattle were yoked to their mangers. I had to be very sure that none of the pigs had sneaked in. The pigs would not have harmed anything in the barn, but a cow's well driven horn might have done serious injury, especially if the pig was soon to farrow.[55]

The watering troughs at the wells were made of half barrels that had to be emptied every evening after the stock had been watered. If this were not done, I had to chop out the ice before using them again. Nature was not cooperative.

After evening chores at the barn, I returned to the house, had supper, ricked fuel in the woodbox, and filled the water barrels for the next day. The water was carried in pails hung from a yoke over my neck. After the wells froze, I had to haul water from Dalliba pit. The old mare did not like the trip to the pit, as she demonstrated by

---

[55] Give birth; the term specifically applies to pigs and originally meant "young pig."

shaking her head, shying, and looking sharp-eyed when I started to harness her. But that was our job and we had to do it.

Before retiring I went to inspect the barn to see that everything was shipshape. It was then about eight o'clock and I was so tired that I went to bed almost at once. I never brought home any school work, even for Saturdays and Sundays. Of course we had ordinary kerosene lamps that did not provide much light, but I was too tired for studying and reading. My teachers were generous and understanding. Again before going to bed, I sliced shavings and chopped fine kindling that I placed between the legs of the box-stove. Grandmother put a few matches on a chair nearby.

If Grandmother was not too busy with her wool-spinning, knitting, carpet-making, quilting, or clothes patching, she was waiting to chat with me for a while. Regardless of what she did, she was always anxious to help me. After a short evening, we said our Rosary together and kissed goodnight.

Stepping to one side in her bedroom, I prepared for bed, then climbed up the stairway, pushed up the trap door, dropped it back again, and scooted into my cold but well-furnished bed of woolen blankets and buffalo robes. I was soon warm and sleeping soundly.

To one who has always lived in a modern home with gas and electricity, my boyhood home must seem hard to endure, but when I reminisce I feel otherwise, because I had the bountiful affection and love of my grandmother.

The Land All Around

The forests and swamps that surrounded the farm were rich larders for supplementing food raised on the farm. As with the farm work, considerable effort was needed to bring that food to the table. Wilfred learned to hunt, fish, and trap animals, and to find berries for his grandmother to make into her delicious pies—or to eat fresh.

Blueberries

The broad down[56] on the north side of the plateau had long been despoiled of its primeval forest, and a thick second growth of bushes and of maple, birch, poplar, and balsam saplings had taken over. Among the small patches of stumps left from the first forest, blueberry bushes thrived, producing unusually large, luscious fruit, which the people I knew called "huckleberries"; we did not know there was a difference. The blueberry bush usually grows no more than knee high, and to pick the berries requires stooping, but the true huckleberry bush is tall, and we had to pull the branches down. The patches were easily accessible, and Grandmother and I spent many entrancing hours together picking the berries.

When the frosts did not destroy the blooms, the crop was bountiful, and the blueberry crop was a matter of grave concern to us. We picked them not only for our own consumption but also to sell to buyers for distant markets. They were of social importance as well. "Did the frost damage the blueberry flowers?" was a query at gatherings in the spring. Then there were reminiscences of blueberry picking parties the year before.

---

[56] Treeless hillside.

I well remember how anxious I was that there be blueberries. I would venture alone along the fence down the long hill to the woods where the forest floor was traced with the paths of cattle and deer, down to the blueberry bushes.

So anxious was I that we have blueberries that my first inspection was before the leaves on the bushes had fully grown. Among the little curly leaves, beady clumps extended up. By and by, those little beads began to open and out came blooms that looked so much like tiny lilies of the valley.

"Frost last night?" Grandmother asked anxiously when we arose.

The French pancakes and maple syrup were ready—a hurried breakfast. No time for shoes. Out around the woodshed, cold dew splashed my bare legs. Over the brow of the hill I ran through the meadow of the down. Across the valley I saw the sheer granite cliffs and the forest-covered bluffs—the Huron Mountains. Through the barbed wire fence, along the path in the woods—down—down to the blueberry patches. The blossoms were waxy and erect, and like playful eyes, they seemed to wink.

Day after day I made my inspection. The clusters grew, and the danger from the frost passed. About mid-June the tiny blooms had turned to beads of green, and with the passing days, the beads became red, then purple, then....

One morning, as I approached the blueberry patch, a partridge flushed from among the bushes. Blueberries. At first one here, one there, a few—each firmly held in its cluster. I carefully detached one and held it between my lips and felt the seeds. Pressing among the waxy leaves, I picked here and there, placing each berry in the hollow of my hand until I had a little pile of blue. I hurried back along the path and up the hill.

"See!" I exclaimed as I held out my hand for Grandmother's inspection. I rolled the berries into her hand. She relished each berry separately.

Each succeeding morning after the berries began to blue, I made my inspection of the blueberry patches, taking with me a small tin cup into which I progressively put more and more berries. After the cup could be filled, I resorted to taking a quart-and-a-half pail, enough for each person in the household to have a dessert of blueberries in milk with a bit of sugar. One day there were enough for a pie—Grandmother's blueberry pie oozing with syrupy blue juice seeping through the flaky crust.

Finally, the blueberries were ready to be picked in quantity. On that afternoon, Grandmother had been particularly busy with her work. She skimmed the cream from the earthen bowls, she baked bread and cookies, and, for the men, she put a crock of cold, boiled, brined pork on a shelf in the icehouse. Upstairs, a long table was covered with a clean, white canvas cloth on which we would spread a thin layer of berries for drying. The grape baskets were dusted and lined with paper. Everything was in readiness for the morning; nothing that could be done was left for blueberry-picking day.

Evening and the dark came slowly. To bed early, but before retiring, we went out beyond the small grove of maples by the house to see the sky. The stars were twinkling and the moon was shining. Dew was heavy on the grass. The northern lights streaked high above the Huron Mountains. All was well for our first blueberry picking. An exciting and anxious night passed slowly. I tiptoed to the south window. My uncles were sleeping soundly, with peaceful breathing. The moon was nearing the western horizon, and in the eastern sky I saw lightning. Back I went to my bed to wait—wait.

Dawn. The two men rose, dressed quietly, and went to the stable to feed the horses and then to the barn for the milking. I heard the light tread of feet below and the faint clinking of lids and the clunk of the farmer stove in the kitchen. I kicked away the bed covers, dressed hurriedly, and ran downstairs. I looked for things to do to help with the morning work—arranging two earthen bowls to be filled with the strained milk, replenishing the fire with split wood, filling the pails with water from the well, wiping the dishes and putting them in the cupboard.

"Has the dew fallen yet?" asked Grandmother.

With bare feet and shanks, I ran to the field a few steps from the door. The grass was dusty.

The coolness of the June dawn was warming under the brilliant sun—not a cloud in the heavens. Grandmother fitted a light scarf on her head and adjusted her apron; she was ready. Each of us hooked a basket containing a dumper—a small pail—over an arm. My basket also had sandwiches and cookies. Out we went, anxiously, expectantly, through the field, along the fence on one side of the big maple grove. Grasshoppers darted. The sheep watched us from their paddocks. In the flat-bottomed valley below, I saw the alder-lined creeks, hay marshes, thick, dark evergreens, and the bluffs beyond. At the fence I raised the bottom barbed wire and Grandmother crawled under and then spread two wires for me. A few more steps down a path and we were in a blueberry patch. Several partridges flushed and disappeared in the foliage of the thick, young trees.

Blueberries grow and ripen fast. There were many more ripe ones that morning than the morning before, and the berries had swelled. Fine big bunches—each a handful at the end of a strong, slender stem—pointed upward invitingly. I had already noted where the nicest berries and the largest clumps were. Grandmother followed me to the spot, where we stopped and examined the berries. We smiled at each other and commented on this year's fine crop. I put my basket under a small balsam and the other within Grandmother's reach. She pushed into the bushes and began to pick. We used dumpers, which we filled and then emptied into the basket. Being a child, I was less patient and spent time looking for the larger berries. Grandmother always picked more berries than I did. I always left the best patches for her.

As careful as we tried to be, we pulled leaves along with the berries and mixed them in the dumpers. To get rid of the leaves, I would stand on a stump or large rock and let the berries roll out of a dumper and down to the basket on the ground. As they dropped, Grandmother fanned them with my straw hat, or sometimes a strong breeze was sufficient without fanning. The moving air caused the leaves to fall to one side of the basket and the berries to the other. Twigs, unfortunately, we had to take out by hand.

When the sun was directly overhead and hot, we stopped for lunch under a balsam tree. I walked to the stream—a branch of the Escanaba River—at the foot of the hill and filled my dumper with the warm, stale, marshy water. Then we sat in the shade at the edge of the blueberry patch and ate our sandwiches of buttered bread with jam made from blueberries picked the year before. Some of it smeared my hands and face, and Grandmother was amused.

My child's exploratory ventures would sometimes take me out of Grandmother's view. Then an affectionate, "Hoo, hoo!" with a reply of, "Hoo, hoo!" assured her that I had not strayed too far.

As the afternoon progressed and the air began to cool, the mosquitoes, deer flies, and no-seeums (very tiny flies) began to annoy us. The deer flies were not so numerous; however, they hit hard and bit severely. A common saying was that they bit off chunks, then went to a stump to eat them. And those mosquitoes—big northerners—were awful with their long stingers. They left such big welts, though we could manage to wave and brush them away. However, the no-seeums distressed us: they actually got into our skin. When they began to get inside our clothes, they were almost unendurable. We never used any repellent—we didn't know of any. At first Grandmother waved the pests away with her outstretched hand, then she flapped the corner of her apron, finally we spent more time fighting the pests than we employed picking berries.

Down in the valley we might see a deer dodging among the saplings, venturing in the direction of our clover field. Grandmother shook her apron and skirt, stood erect, and arranged her scarf. Dew was forming on the leaves. She leveled the berries in each basket and covered them with paper, pressing the edges down over the sides of the basket where they were fastened by a cord.

I lifted a basket with each hand, and Grandmother, carrying the dumpers, led the way, for she would have to pull the hazel branches aside to prevent them from striking and scratching my face and hands. The air was quickly cooling as the shadows darkened the woods. Deer tracks packed the damp earth in the path. A snowshoe rabbit in his gray summer coat lunged for cover. A partridge cock drummed.

We struggled up the path supremely elated with our companionship and satisfied with the day's harvest. Suddenly, the fence stopped us at the edge of the field. We struggled between the strands of wire and then we were in the fluffy-headed timothy and the blossoming red clover. As we climbed the hill, the sheep followed along the fence, converging at the gate. Grandmother stopped and inhaled long breaths, hooked up one corner of her apron, and fanned herself. Side by side, we reached the house.

The evening's work would presently be upon us.

Rest was short. A drink of cool milk and probably a cookie each, and upstairs we went with our baskets filled with berries. On the table we had already prepared, Grandmother poured some of the berries from each basket, beginning at one end of the table and letting them form a sort of windrow.[57] As Grandmother spread the berries in a thin layer, I picked tiny twigs, coarse stems, and bits of leaves. Until the blueberries were through oozing, Grandmother and I would go upstairs each morning, stand on opposite sides of the table, and shake the cloth several times to move the berries so they would dry thoroughly

Each day of blueberry season, we added to the store. The blueberries in the lower part of each basket had begun to mash and ooze by the time we got home. The members of the household who wanted to eat blueberries right away—and that was every member—had all they wanted. Part of the surplus was made into jam and the remainder was preserved.

---

[57] A long line of raked hay or sheaves of grain laid out to dry in the wind.

Trapping Fish

T he men of the household and I, and later I alone, trapped game fish during the fish runs while the water of the spring freshets[58] was receding. One place I fished was Delongchamp Creek, which flowed into the East Branch of the Escanaba River, the longest river in the Upper Peninsula.

Here the men constructed a dam in the river by placing two stout poles side by side across the stream. A sheet of corrugated iron salvaged from one of the iron mines and large stones to keep the poles in place completed the dam. In the middle they cut a square hole to hold the fishtrap.

Our fish trap was made of common wood and allowed the fish to enter but not escape. The fish trap was held in place by water pressure and stones. We checked it each morning before breakfast to make sure no town boys got to it first.

Fish-trapping lasted only a few days because the water level soon went down and the fish stopped running in large numbers. Also, some of the fish—especially suckers—were not good to eat after the water became warm and stale.

---

[58] Stream overflow caused, in this case, by snow melting in the spring.

While the run was at its best, the trap caught a lot of fish. There were speckled trout, perch, bass, bullheads, and other kinds of fish of which I did not know the names, and of course there was the lowly sucker. We usually caught two gunnysacks full of fish each morning, which was much more than the household could eat. We gave the surplus to our relatives and friends in town. It was fun to see the fish tumbling out of the gunnysacks into two large tubs partially filled with cold water fresh from the well and to see them dart against the sides and circle. After breakfast, Grandmother and I sorted the fish, keeping the trout, perch, and bass.

A wooden fish trap lasted a couple of springs. After my uncles left home to marry, I tended to the fish-trapping. Eventually fish traps became obsolete because game laws prohibited their use.

The gang of kids to which I belonged had another method for trapping fish that was exciting and, we thought, quite ingenuous. Two of us would take a bag and sew the mouth around a barrel hoop[59] to keep it open. In the little creek that flows through Champion, one of the boys would stand in the water, brace his legs against the bank, and hold the trap between his legs. Another boy would walk upstream and poke under the banks with a pole, then, with his feet, drive the fish before him. When a fish dashed into the sack, it was lifted out and dumped on the bank.

---

[59] A metal band that holds together the staves of a barrel or cask.

We could "guddle fish"—the name for the sport—only when the water was warm and quite low, so most of our catch consisted of suckers.

Salting Deer

Before there were deer conservation laws, we hunted deer any time and in any way we wanted. Shooting deer began about the last days of July after they had recovered from the hard winter and become fleshy enough to make good venison. We also waited so that the fawns could remain with the does until they were weaned.

The most effective method for getting within shooting range of deer was by enticing them to a salt lick, which they visited at dusk and in the night. Shooting deer at a salt lick was neither sport nor hunting—it was just plain slaughter—like shooting cattle in a barnyard.

To establish a good salt lick required more than one season. A deer-stalker started a salt lick by scattering a lot of salt on the roots of a large stump or fallen tree at the edge of a hay marsh or meadow where deer came at night to feed. More salt was added from time to time. Deer soon found the salt, which they crave. If the stalker did not bring enough salt, the animals crunched at the wood.

Within good shooting range, the stalker built a hideout to wait for his quarry. There were three kinds of hideouts: a small hole in a hillside covered with branches, a lean-to made of large branches propped against the roots of an upturned tree, and a scaffold in a branchy treetop, usually a large hemlock, tamarack, or white pine.

Because of the deer's extraordinarily keen sense of hearing and smell, the stalker could not make much noise to drive away the mosquitoes, deer flies, and other pests. Stalking deer was not much fun.

The deer came along their trails very cautiously and stealthily. The slightest noise startled them, causing them to leap and dash back into the thick brush. Then the stalker had to start his wait all over. If a buck was startled, he whiff-whistled very loudly so that no other deer came that evening. A rather amusing annoyance was squirrels, partridges, and rabbits bounding around the dry leaves and making more noise than the deer.

When a stalker anticipates seeing a deer, he sometimes gets "buck fever"—his breathing becomes labored, his heart thumps, and he is tense. I have heard of hunters not only fainting but dying from heart attacks caused by buck fever. It's not suddenly seeing a deer but the waiting anxiously that causes buck fever. Anyone who has not hunted deer cannot imagine a stalker's feeling when, expecting a deer, a squirrel comes hopping through the dry leaves.

I had buck fever many times. On one occasion I emptied my rifle without once hitting a fine buck as it loped by. I am certain that most fatalities during deer-hunting season are the result of buck fever.

After killing a deer, I dragged it at once into the bushes, built a smudge to keep away the annoying flies, and dressed it. I hung it from a tree until I could return later in the evening.

I often did not get a deer, but it wasn't unusual for me to be tramping home after dark and startle a buck, which would go crashing through the bushes whiff-whistling loudly.

Snowshoe Rabbits

I f you have not seen a snowshoe rabbit, you have missed seeing the most interesting member of the hare species.[60] They live where there are long winters and much snow and cold.

The name fits it perfectly. It is snow-white in winter and gray in summer, so that its color imitates the surroundings very well. It is difficult to see a snowshoe rabbit during either season unless nature plays it a mean trick: if there is not much snow, the white coat makes it easy prey for man and owls and hawks, and if snow covers the ground before its fur has turned white, it is also easily visible.

The snowshoe rabbit is well equipped for deep snow. Its hind feet are long, hairy, and well-padded—perfect snowshoes. Although it rarely ventures out of the swamp in which it was born,

---

[60] The snowshoe is actually a hare, not a rabbit. Because hares live above ground, their babies (called "leverets") are more prepared for survival than are rabbit babies (called "kittens"), which are born underground. Rabbits are born hairless with their eyes closed, while hares are born fully furred with their eyes open. Hares' bodies and hind legs are generally longer.

it keeps on the move at night. It must keep warm, find tender bark to eat, and stay out of the reach of its enemies.

Unlike the cottontail, which hides in holes and hollow logs, the snowshoe rabbit likes to hide in thick underbrush with an abundance of small evergreen trees whose branches slant down to the ground. During summer breeding time, the snowshoe rabbit is safe from hunters, but when the snow begins to cover the ground, its life is in peril.

I had a lot of fun hunting snowshoe rabbits, alone, with hounds, and with snares.

Snowshoe rabbit-hunting dogs were especially trained for that purpose. A snowshoe rabbit will not move unless the hunters or the dogs are very near, and it usually bounds away before that happens. However, a good snowshoe rabbit-hunting dog does a fine job and adds greatly to the sport.

With my dog, I would go to a swamp and look for tracks. When the hound found a rabbit, he howled and gave chase. The rabbit took off, going round and round and zigzagging, staying just far enough ahead to stay out of danger. If I was in the right place, the dog drove the rabbit past me. I enjoyed watching rabbits as they streaked for short distances when the dog drew near. When it thought itself out of danger, the rabbit sat up and looked back, its long ears sticking straight up. Shooting a snowshoe rabbit while it was sitting was easy. Hitting it as it streaked by was real excitement.

After the snowshoe rabbit was killed, the hound came up, smelled his quarry, and looked up for orders. If told to do so, he went in quest of another. I hung the game from my belt or threw it into a canvas sack over my shoulder.

I hunted with dogs not only for the meat but also for the excitement. I used a snare when I was just after the meat. It wasn't sporting, because if the snare was set properly, the rabbit didn't have a chance.

Snowshoe rabbits don't like to leave their swamps, so their paths through the snow are well packed and become quite deep and narrow. Those paths necessarily pass between bushes and saplings that are just far enough apart to let the rabbit pass between them. I set my snares in those narrow passages.

I made each snare out of braided picture wire formed into a miniature lasso and hung from a short stick across the trail. The loop was large enough to permit the rabbit's head to pass through, but not its forepaws. As it hopped along, the rabbit poked its head through the wire, and the loop, like a lasso, closed around its neck. The rabbit choked and, after a struggle, strangled.

Snaring was done almost entirely by boys and was very easy, as all you had to do was set the snare and come back later.

The meat of the snowshoe rabbit is delicious. The hares have big hind quarters and loins, and the pink meat is juicy and clear, like young chicken. Grandmother spread thin slices of salt pork or bacon over the pieces and roasted them in the oven. Our Cornish[61] friends liked them in rabbit pie and pasties.[62]

---

[61] Immigrants from Cornwall, England.
[62] Small meat pies that the Cornish introduced to the Upper Peninsula.

A Winter Day in the Woods

A late November Saturday evening and one of my uncles had come down from the logging camp, relieving me of my Sunday chores. I had been hoping for such good fortune, so I made preparations to go hunting the next day.

I took my 30-40 box magazine Winchester rifle from a bracket on the wall of the downstairs closet and, with enough cartridges, placed it on the end of the kitchen table. Anticipating thawing temperature, soggy ground, and watery swamps, I greased my hunting shoepacks well and placed them near the boxstove. My thick woolen socks, toque, and mackinaw lay on a chair. Grandmother wrapped thick slices of well-buttered and mustard-seasoned sandwiches and some boiled pork hocks.

Outside, the air was still, and large fluffy snowflakes floated to the earth. Under the cover of buffalo robes I slept soundly in the cold upstairs.

Before daybreak, Grandmother's broomstick knocked against the ceiling. I gathered my clothes, lifted the trapdoor in the floor, and rushed into the warming living room. Grandmother had returned to her bed, so I dressed at the side of the reddening boxstove. She had set out slices of bread, cold meat, and a cupcake. Tea was warming on the stove. While I was filling my mouth with

121

one hand and dressing with the other, I watched the clock, for I wanted to be away before sunrise.

Finally, I pulled the knapsack straps over my head, and grabbing my rifle and shells, hurried to the door and out. The horizon was lightening, the air was delightfully calm, and snow drifted down. During the night, enough snow had fallen to cover old tracks, so I would be able to distinguish new ones. I turned north through the field to the brow of a long down. Never had I been more thrilled with that view before me: the snow-blanketed fields still gray in the dawn, the lacy branches of the maples, birches, and poplars, the sagging, snow-laden boughs of the spruces, balsams, and jack pines in the valley below. Beyond the valley lay the forest of black-plumed white pines, the big hardwoods, and the challenging bluffs.

I descended the hill to the fields and crossed to the rock-lined fence at the edge where a weasel had left its little paw prints as it hopped up the hill in the direction of our barn and chicken coop. A flock of snowbirds perched like great beads along the fence wire, then flitted away among the snowflakes. The fence posts were topped with little igloos of snow.

A few steps into the thicket and I was on a trail to the Escanaba River. Snow-covered, willowy branches of hazel and chokecherry bushes drooped, dropping their snowy burdens at the slightest touch or quiver of air.

I strode down the hill to a hump overlooking the bank of the river. The narrow stream was not entirely frozen, but ice and snow met in the deep narrow places. Shallow water gurgled beneath. Cautiously I footed my way across the dam we had created for our fish trap and crossed to the long narrow marsh.

The marsh was soggy and the snow lay level over the wild-hay tufts. Stumbling through and sinking in the muck, I recalled the struggle to harvest the wild hay. A few steps down the slope to the east, I arrived at the old corduroy road over which pulpwood had been hauled on sleighs from the lumber camps. With hopping and irregular steps I followed that road to a small plateau where I stopped at the jumbled remnants of a pulpwood-cutter's shanty. A porcupine, up on its hind feet and supported by its tail, crunched the salty, smashed table.

I tossed a small stick at the porky and it glanced in my direction, blinked, flopped on its belly in the soft snow, and stretched its spiny tail to give me a smack. I touched the porky's back with the muzzle of my rifle. Menacingly, it sent up its black-tipped quills. I stood quietly until the porky blinked, then pressed its front paws tightly over its nose; its tail quivered. On a branch of a large red birch, another porcupine nibbled the wintergreen-flavored bark.

Leaving the porkies to their winter forage, I started up the side of the little, jack pine-covered plateau. I found hoof prints that told me that during the night, two deer—a buck and a doe—had crossed through the bushes. From the entrance of what had been a large marsh, I heard the gurgling of the water flowing over a beaver dam.

Although the winter was quite well advanced and the beavers were usually in their house at that time of year, I saw tracks and signs that they had been inspecting and repairing their dam. The water in the pond had not frozen solidly enough to carry my weight, so I did not venture to visit the igloo-like beaver houses.

Following the right bank of the marsh, I arrived at the uprooted stump against which I had once built a hideout to stalk deer at a salt lick, but now the beaver dam had covered the salt lick with water.

Now I entered the great forest-covered bluffs. The giant white pines towered among the hardwoods—maple and red birch. Paul Bunyan's garden. My mind could not then imagine that within a few years, the entire region would be devastated and laid waste.[63]

Following the side of the ridge, I reached the end of the marsh to enter a large swamp wooded with spruce, tamarack, and cedar. Snowshoe rabbit trails were deep in the snow. I continued along the little creek where on the bank I saw the tracks of minks as they went in and out of holes under the eroded roots, fallen trees, and overhanging banks. Later in the winter I would run a trapline[64] for them.

---

[63] According to Wilfred, the lumber companies cut down all of the virgin white pine forests.

[64] A circuit of animal traps.

A Winter Day in the Woods

I had entered into the evergreen swamp only a short distance when I began to see more deer tracks and the frayed bark on some small trees where the bucks had rubbed their itching antlers. Alerted, I was on the lookout for a shot. I took the Winchester from my shoulder, wiped the barrel, and examined the muzzle to make sure it was not clogged with snow or dirt. I worked the lever several times and injected five cartridges into the magazine and one into the chamber of the barrel. I began to stalk and peer behind trees, upturned roots, and clumps of brush, avoiding stepping on dry twigs. The trees were thick and the snow-laden branches made excellent cover for the deer.

As I watched, I was startled by the loud whiff-whistle blast of a buck coming from a thick clump of small evergreens behind the roots of an upturned pine. I jumped aside in time to see the buck lunge into the thicket and disappear.

I went to the spot where the buck had been lying and saw there had been two deer—a doe with the buck. My only interest in the doe was that the buck might return, for it was rutting[65] season. I had not gone far into the thicket when I encountered more deer tracks in crisscrossing trails, which confused me. But I had noticed a particular distinguishing mark in the track of the buck that I chose to follow: one of his hooves turned outward and the halves of the hoof were spread unusually wide apart. That buck would be easy to track.

---

[65] Mating.

125

I followed it through the swamp and along the edge of the evergreens where the ground rises to the ridge. The underbrush and saplings were not thick there, and the open view made poor cover for the deer. The tracks showed that, when the deer reached the end of the lake, it had turned to follow the western shore. Near the lake I climbed a prostrate trunk for an extended view. The bark had decayed, loosened, and fallen, and the snow made the surface of the trunk so slick that it was difficult to keep my balance. As I teetered, a buck startled me with a whiff-whistle. I shook, sweated, slipped, and breathed hard: buck fever.

There was stifling silence, then suddenly the deer crashed through the brush with a terrific whistling blast. I glanced aside and, almost at my elbow, the buck stood with bulging eyes, its ears pointing ahead. It was trigger-poised to spring. I pulled the hammer and raised the rifle to my shoulder. Before I could take aim, a great snowflake floated and rested on the rear sight. I blew at the snowflake and leaned my head forward to aim. The buck jerked its nose up, pressed the antlers back along its neck, sprang a long, high hop, and disappeared. Before I could recover from my buck fever, my great hunting prize was well up the ridge, whiff-whistling and contemptuously waving its flag.[66]

---

[66] When a white-tailed deer runs away, it hoists its tail, revealing the white underside.

I rushed to its tracks and was delighted to see that they were from the buck I had been following. My pursuit continued.

The buck reached the top of the ridge, then followed it for some distance. I began to worry: if it went in the direction of Round Lake, I would be enticed farther and farther from home. I did not care to be so far in the bluffs when dark took over. I hoped the buck would circle the lake and return to the swamp.

As the afternoon wore on, the buck stopped more often and its whiff-whistles became louder and more desperate. I saw it more often, but not often enough for a shot.

Approaching the north end of the ridge, the buck came across the fresh tracks of a doe walking in the direction of Long Lake. The buck brushed the snow with its nose and slowed down. During rutting season, especially toward the end, bucks tire more easily and become more reckless.

As I went over the ridge, I almost stopped to shoot at a flock of partridges feeding in a large red birch, but I had a rifle, and a deer is what I wanted, so I continued on, following the tracks down the ridge. The big spruce swamp at the end of Long Lake was just ahead and the trail led into it. There were more and more deer tracks, a sign that they were yarding-up.[67] I spotted the deformed hoof tracks.

---

[67] Huddling together for warmth.

The deer in the swamp had begun their winter feeding, hoofing moss from dead trees, nibbling twigs. Suddenly the buck's whiff-whistle startled me. I saw where a pair of deer had been lying under the low bough of a spruce. The doe went in one direction, the buck toward the lake. I followed the buck to the watery marsh and saw it had sunk in the muck and dragged itself. I knew the morass was dangerous and that I should avoid crossing there, but I followed anyway. When I jumped across the little creek, I missed the bank and fell on my stomach, my feet flopping in the water.

I pulled myself out and hurried to high ground—feeling terrible. What time was it? I didn't have a watch, but my stomach told me that the day was well along. I gobbled my bread-and-butter sandwiches and cold hock, but I couldn't stand still long or my wet feet grew cold, heavy, and painful. Following that buck had ceased to be a thrill, but I kept on.

The deer tracks led up the ridge. While ascending, I was startled again by that whiff-whistle. At the top of a ridge I saw the buck had turned to watch my approach. Down the hill, a flash of the flag, and the buck disappeared in the evergreens. Another whiff-whistle. More deer tracks and more crashing brush.

The buck was following a zigzag course as it sought a hiding place to give me the slip. That damned buck! It emerged from the swamp into the narrow marsh and creek near the end of the lake, loped over the stream and looked back at me over its shoulder. What a disdaining expression! I lost precious time hurrying along the creek to shallower water and firmer banks, but I could not have stood another soaking.

I took up the buck's trail again as it went around a little ridge that reached the shore of the lake. Below was another thick swamp. From the top of a fallen tree I could see the south end of Long Lake at my left. Whiff-whistle—the buck rushed past me! I slipped, regained my footing, and as I looked ahead, there was the buck's rump and its antlers showing above the brush, its white flag waving, its legs poised to bolt. I wiped the sight of my rifle, raised the butt to my shoulder, aimed, and fired.

Down flapped the flag as the buck lunged and disappeared.

Jumping from the tree, I rushed to the tracks and saw blood where its right hind hoof had dragged in the snow. On I pressed for another shot, but again it out-witted me. The low spruce branches obstructed my view. The distance between us was shrinking. Again and again, the buck rushed ahead, stopped, and looked back—but never long enough for me to get a shot.

At the end of the ridge, staggering, the buck entered the big, dark swamp between the south end of Long Lake and the marsh.

If a deer is wounded, it is best to leave it alone until it lies down and stiffens, so I stopped at the edge of the swamp to examine snowshoe rabbit trails. One day I might come back to set snares for them. My feet again grew cold and stiffened, so on I went.

Behind the upturned roots of a fallen spruce I saw my quarry lying in the snow. It was shaking its head and struggling to stand. It looked at me, I imagined, pleadingly.

A well-aimed rifle sent a bullet between the antlers into the head. The chase was ended.

Without delay I dressed my game, then with a small rope from my knapsack, I dragged it head-first to the edge of the bluffs near the place where I had entered that morning.

I hurried home so that I could return that night for my buck. After changing into dry clothes and shoes, I hitched the old mare to the jumper, then drove down the road past the Pasco Mine, down across the Escanaba River, and followed the old corduroy pulpwood road to my prize, loaded it up, and returned home. Exhausted but happy and satisfied, I was ready to do the evening chores.

Education

Until he was in first grade, Wilfred spoke French but almost no English. His stepgrandfather spoke a little English but his grandmother none at all. His stepgrandfather was illiterate while his grandmother read and wrote in French. His aunts and uncles spoke English fairly well, but their formal education had stopped at about the fourth grade. His grandparents encouraged his pursuit of an education.

School Days

I attended three schools, all in Champion and all about one and a half miles from my home on the farm. The road to town was mostly in open country on a plateau. In winter, bitterly cold winds made travel unpleasant, but going to school in summer was delightful.

When I was little, someone drove me by horse and cutter in the winter, but as I got older, I drove myself or walked. The roads were obliterated most of the time and the packed snow was very unpleasant and made traveling slow. I traveled cross-country on skis made from barrel staves or on snowshoes, cutting across fields and always trying to avoid the wind. My skiing was not very good, but I did quite well with the excellent snowshoes that belonged to one of my uncles.

I was never absent except during occasional severe snow storms, when the drifts were so deep that a horse could not easily get through. I was, however, frequently late. When I was late, my classmates and teachers were very pleased to see me, and they apparently admired my fortitude. I am certain that I was foolhardy to venture so far from home on those bitterly cold days and in such sweeping blizzards. Grandmother's prayers protected me.

I attended first grade in a small frame building near the downtown depot. The building was divided into a classroom of ample size and a narrow entrance hall across the front. Large, round woodstoves in the hall and classroom furnished sufficient heat. On nice days during warm weather we sat among the gravestones and under the trees in the cemetery a few yards up the hill. When the weather kept us indoors, those of us who carried our lunches ate while sitting on the floor around the stove.

It was while sitting by that stove that I was first impressed with the horrible effects on people of an economic depression—the Panic of 1893.[68] My home was on what was considered the most prosperous farm thereabout. I always had enough to eat and I was comfortably clothed. In contrast, other children at my school suffered from an excessive condition of want. Day after day children brought their lunches of cold, slightly salted mashed potatoes in small, sometimes rusty pails. I had good bread and butter sandwiches; cold, boiled, brined pork; boiled or roasted beef; boiled eggs; raw onions; and fresh cabbage. An occasional apple shone like a rare jewel. And, of course, I had Grandmother's delicious cookies. I thought the other children eyed me enviously and sometimes contemptuously. Their poverty affected me so deeply that I shared my lunch with them. When we played games, I

---

[68] The worst economic depression the United States had experienced up to that time.

was often favored. It was only much later that I realized that some of the other children interpreted my sharing as bribes.

My first teacher was Miss Pullin, who was rather plump, pretty, understanding, and loveable. I must have been a good pupil, because I was skipped to the second grade before finishing the first.

The next school that I attended was a two-room structure that stood a few yards behind a large building known as the high school. The two rooms were separated by a long, narrow hall with hooks on the walls where we children hung our wraps. The first grade was in one room, and the second and third grades were in the other.

Photo courtesy of the town of Champion.

On the right is the second elementary school Wilfred attended; on the left is the third elementary school/high school.

The superintendent of our school until 1900 was J.B. Montgomery. He was a large, athletic man with long red whiskers who thoroughly believed in the rule of terrorism. He was very cruel and he seemed to enjoy punishing the boys. He was a bully, causing the children, and most of the parents, to thoroughly despise him. I was the victim of his wrath a number of times.

Montgomery was also commissioner of schools for the county, so he sometimes left town by train. Walking to the railroad station took him within sight of the school. When the large boys spotted him, they would shout, "There goes J.B.!" That was the signal for disorder in the entire school for that day. The teachers were very compassionate on those days.

One morning, Miss Elizabeth Wright, the assembly room supervisor, had completed roll call and directed the pupils, "Pass to your classes."

As we stood to leave, the door swung open and J. B. strode into the room. His face was pink putty and pudgy, and his anger-clenched mouth pushed his broomy whiskers out. His eyes bulged and glared.

We slumped back into our seats.

"Henry, you will go to my office—now!"

Sorrowfully, we watched Henry walk out with J. B. following. The door latch clicked loudly. The office where he took Henry was right next door.

The pupils glanced at Miss Wright and then at the floor.

"Take off your coat," we heard J.B. snap.

The children froze in their seats and listened intently.

"Come here!" The terrorizing command came through the door as though it were open. Except for deep breathing, the silence was stifling.

Miss Wright stood, turned to face the front of the room, and put her handkerchief to her eyes.

Suddenly a long roar broke the calm. "Ow-ow-ow-o-o-o!!!"

A loud thud, the office door slammed, and footsteps ran down the stairs.

At recess we all rushed out and the boys soon found Henry hiding in the loft of the old barn at one corner of the school lot.

"Tell us what happened!" we begged. And this is what Henry recounted.

With his powerful hands, J. B. had grabbed Henry by the scruff of the neck and jammed him—head first—between his tree-trunk legs. Henry had submitted meekly and waited for the slams of the strap.

J. B. reached to the edge of his desk, grabbed the large strap, readjusted Henry's butt, and tightened the pants to enhance the impact of the blows.

Henry turned his face up to watch the motion of J. B.'s hand and the strap.

Slowly, so as to inflict all the agony possible, J. B. straightened, extended his arm high and swung the strap back, but before

137

he could start the strap on its downward swing, Henry jammed the full length of a long pin that he had concealed for the occasion into J. B.'s plump behind.

In the sudden agony, J. B. had uncontrollably slammed the strap to the floor as Henry escaped out the door.

For some time after his defeat by Henry, we noticed that J. B. sat on the edge of his chair, and from then on, it seemed, he had a fear of sharp things, and it is believed that he never used his strap that way again.

When I reached fourth grade, I started attending school in the high school building, which consisted of a basement and three stories. The basement contained the heating plant and two large rooms, one for boys and one for girls, where we ate our lunches and which we used for recreation during winter months. The second and third stories of two rooms each were for the fourth, fifth, sixth, and seventh grades. The third story was for the eighth grade and the high school.

The immigrant settlers in Champion came directly from their native lands, and each group spoke its particular language and conformed to and observed customs and traditions brought from abroad. The members of each group tended to live together, but the school was the merging place for the children—the melting pot. Nearly all the children brought dinner lunches to school, and they exchanged nationality items of food with delight. I usually had boiled eggs to exchange for a [Cornish meat] pasty.

In high school, I decided to play hooky one afternoon, something I had never done before. I was lonely and just got tired of going. The heat was oppressive and the air was stifling. It seemed like a good afternoon to hide in the shade and be free from school.

While the children were at play, I sneaked down the town road and around the low ridge to the railroad track, then to the old empty and decaying buildings of the Keystone Mine. From there I could watch the world go by. I went to the barn and climbed the ladder to the loft. Several cows lay on the earth floor chewing their cuds. The bells hanging from their necks rang monotonously. The stench from the manure soon became unpleasant.

Sitting in a window, I looked over the landscape. An occasional noise from the highway sent me scampering temporarily to a darkened corner.

The fear of being seen, the solitude, the heat, and the stench became more and more oppressive as the afternoon passed. Not having a timepiece, I waited and waited for the recess bell to ring. Finally I heard the children playing, then the ringing of the bell calling them in. The afternoon dragged and dragged. Finally, I left the barn and, following the edge of the woods, went up the track toward the school and waited—and waited—for school to be dismissed. Guiltily, I walked back to the town road to join the passing youngsters.

That evening the supper was stale, especially when Grandmother looked at me.

In the spring of 1902, my sophomore year in high school, I was not doing well, nor did I want to. I had quit school to work in the North Mine, an iron mine about a mile from home. I was sixteen then—tall, gangly, smart (so I thought). I wanted to earn money and be big. Other boys worked for wages and had money; why not I?

One spring day at the mine, a large chunk of iron ore fell on the back of my hand and tore a long gash. The wound was stitched and bound, and all there was for me to do was to loiter and think. Not going to school made me the envy of the other boys of my age. But what did I have that they should envy me for?

Grandmother had scolded me severely, though kindly, for having left school. What to do? Should I please her or just be stubborn? Oh, how I loved and adored her!

At that moment, the three young teachers that made up the high school faculty came to our door: Miss Frances Brown, Miss Mabel Hurst, and Miss Leila McCotter. Those teachers liked me. Why? I don't know. I certainly had not made myself likeable.

At the door, they flattered me, telling me they wanted to pick the little arbutus flowers, now in their spring bloom, and that I knew where all the best ones where. Would I go with them?

The grass was dewy, the red clay in the trails gooey. The Escanaba River overflowed its banks, and the marshes were soaked.

They didn't care. They laughed gaily as we walked to the brow of the down.

"There," I said, pointing. "See beyond the marsh, just across the track? That's where those beautiful arbutus grow. I'll get them for you."

"No, no. We'll go too."

So we went. Down the long hill, through the field to the edge of the woods. Between the barbed wires of the fence.

On we went through the woods, down to the river to the big tree trunk that spanned the stream. We held hands and crossed sideways. On through the swamp, across another fence, stumbling. I carried them piggy-back across a marshy creek until we came to where the deep pink arbutus with their waxy leaves grew in large clustered blooms. Tenderly, we gathered the clusters of sweet-scented blooms, careful not to injure the vines or roots.

We returned by the same route and in the manner in which we had gone. Wet, muddy, happy, we reached the house where Grandmother brewed tea, a very delicious and welcome drink for tired bodies, and served cookies and blueberry jam.

Grandmother could not speak English, but she could under-stand it quite well, and she had great fun listening to their chatter.

I do not know if those teachers had planned the morning's outing to induce me to return to school, but as each of them placed her arm about Grandmother's shoulders and thanked her and as they waved to us as they went southward down the road, I resolved to go back to school for them and for Grandmother and that I would stay. I kept that resolution.

Graduation 1904

F inally, the time had arrived for commencement. One afternoon, Frederick Monical, our high school principal, called me into his office. When I entered, he had my school record on his desk. It was not an impressive record. Mr. Monical came around the desk and put his arm about my waist and said, "Son, you don't have credit enough to graduate. You had only one-and-a-half years of Latin, and you failed in that."

He paused. I stood silently, tears sliding down my cheeks. Life had not been kind to me; I had rebelled, but now I wanted to graduate and I wanted to go to college. Through the window I looked over the valley and across that plateau toward home where I knew Grandmother would knit stockings, mittens, and scarves, and make butter to sell to help me go to college. I wanted to go for her. I had heard much of college and I knew that the three girls in my class planned to attend a state normal school.[69] Not one of my relatives had graduated from high school, much less from college.

Mr. Monical left me and went back to his desk and began running his pencil up and down the record thoughtfully. Then he turned his face up to me—a tall, gangly, thin, six-foot kid, eighteen

---

[69] Teacher-training college.

143

years old—and smiled. "Son, that's a poor record, and you lack credits. However, I believe that you have it in you to make good. I'm going to allow you those credits, and you are going to college if you wish."

I graduated, and after years of hard work, I graduated from the normal school and the University of Michigan with a bachelor's, master's, and finally, fifteen years after Grandmother had passed away, a law degree. She would have been proud.

Time to Part

The eroded, shallow, red earth of the rocky acres had yielded a meager crop. The gray weedy hay was packed in the barn loft. The large hand-bound sheaves of winter wheat had been carefully hauled and stacked in one of the two mows of the long log barn. The ripe and dry precious *pois vert*[70] were safe in the old lean-to by the house. The nights were growing chillier as the days shortened.

Standing at the little gate, with two empty milk pails hanging from my hands, I saw across the open landscape a team of sweating horses—a roan and a bay—pulling a stout wagon. They were going for the last load of grain. After milking the three cows, I returned to the house and placed the wooden pails by the sink.

On one side of the long oilcloth-covered table, Grandmother had set a place for me to eat my supper. I sat at the table deeply dejected. The hunger that I had entered the kitchen with suddenly left me. Tears brimmed in Grandmother's eyes as she stood across the table from me.

"*Soup de pois?*" she whispered, her mouth quivering.

I could not speak, nodded yes.

---

[70] Green peas.

Grandmother ladled some of the soup into a deep plate and set the plate below my downcast face.

My tears dropped into the soup as I ate. Grandmother encircled my confused head with her arms and pressed it to her bosom and kissed me.

The old clock on the living room wall stared at me through the door, its tick-tock calling, "The time is nigh." The sun lit the well-worn rug on which I had spent so many hours sleeping or playing while Grandmother sat working in her rocking chair.

Sweetly, the bells from the little church on the ridge beyond the valley pealed. Grandmother and I faced each other and bowed our heads. We made the sign of the cross and prayed in silence.

My slow ascent of the narrow stairway along the bare wall to my plain but well-kept room was painful, for I realized then that the descent might be my last. I surveyed that room—the straw-padded bed, the plain, yellowing walls, the bare floor. From the open window, I saw again the expanse of autumn-bright.

I descended the stairs and turned into the parlor where in one corner I saw the antique organ. Would I ever hear her play again?

Grandmother was waiting for me in the living room, her finger-polished, black-bead Rosary hanging from her folded hands. We knelt and said the Rosary.

A bundle lay on a chair near the outer door of the kitchen. It contained all the personal effects that were useful for me to take. I lifted that bundle, tucked it under my left arm, and, with my other arm, I embraced Grandmother's shoulders. We stepped down the three wooden steps out the kitchen door and walked to the small open gate of the yard.

Grandmother pressed my prayer book into my hand. In that small prayer book she had inserted a card on which was finely printed a sketch of Notre Dame de Lourdes. At the bottom of the card she had written in French, "*Pitre, priez bien pour moi.*"[71]

Nearly all the money I had earned in the shanties the preceding winter and on the log drives on the Peshekee River in the spring, I had contributed to the household. The remaining coins were in a small pig-bladder purse under my arm. Grandmother and I had counted those coins—they were so few, but I was determined to go, and determination is not valued in coins. We embraced and kissed again, and as we kissed, Grandmother pressed crinkly paper into my hand—two one-dollar bills, probably all she had.

From down the valley in the west, the train whistle blew its warning. I turned and walked away, across the land I knew so well. At the top of the down, I looked back. Grandmother was standing looking in my direction. She was praying. I heard her prayer.

The train whistle blew. The engine's smoke, rising through the trees, was coming nearer.

---

[71] "Peter, pray well for me."

I stood on my tiptoes and stretched. I waved. Then I ran, eyes blurred with tears, through the barbed wire fence, across the gully to the road. I turned to the right and ran.

Afterward

After graduating from high school, Wilfred attended Cleary Business College in Ypsilanti in 1904 and 1905. He returned to Champion and took a job in the office of Consolidated Coal and Lumber Company in Ishpeming. He was a stenographer, janitor, and sometime-helper in the lumber yard for $35 a month, with room and board costing him $5 a week. He kept the job for two months, then quit and returned to the farm.

"My stepgrandfather was very disappointed because I quit my job in Ishpeming, and he became more and more abusive. One evening in August of 1905, I left after telling my grandmother." He bribed the conductor of the evening passenger train with $2 and traveled to Devil's Lake, Wisconsin, where a boyhood friend worked at a summer resort. He began working at the resort, making friends with several other young people there. One evening they boated to a little store at the far end of the lake. "The proprietor played on a cylindrical record phonograph the song 'Where Is My Wandering Boy Tonight.' I cried and went at once to my shack, begged some paper, and wrote to Grandmother. I never ignored her again."

After two weeks, he jumped a train and traveled to St. Paul, Minnesota, where he bounced from job to job, first at the state hatchery, then as a fireman on the Chicago, Milwaukee, and St. Paul Railroad. He added three years to his age to get into fireman school and, he said, was highly recommended by the engineer. "However, I was right handed, and since the shoveling of coal had to be [done] left-handed, I found the work too hard and disagreeable, so I quit."

Wilfred working as a hook-tender, age 22.

He next turned to working in lumber camps, moving on to the Puget Sound area of Washington State.[72] In Washington, he was working for $2.25 a day building skidroads[73] when the San Francisco earthquake "caused wages to skyrocket." He was promoted to hook-tender at $150 a month, including board.

Maxime died in 1907. Wilfred returned home that summer to help his grandmother and took up his familiar chores, but he returned to Puget Sound in the fall.

In 1908, his grandmother was removed from her home by her sons, Fred and John, who usurped her farm, and placed in a house in Champion. Twelve-year-old Margret "Eva" Hamel, one of her daughter Mary Nellie's many children, was taken out of school and lived with Celina Delongchamp to care for her.

In 1911, Wilfred enrolled at Northern State Normal for a two-year course of study, graduating in 1912.

---

[72] In his retirement years, he wrote two books about logging: *Puget Sound Lumberjack*, and *Logging in the Huron Mountains*. Some stories were published separately in periodicals such as *Minnesota History Quarterly*. He also wrote some pieces about mining in Michigan, as that was an important part of the community in which he was raised and he had occasionally worked for mining companies. The mining stories were published in a daily newspaper, *Mining Journal*, "Upper Michigan's Largest Daily."

[73] Roads made of logs for hauling timber.

On March 6, 1912, his beloved grandmother died of Bright's disease[74] at age sixty one.

Over the next several years, he taught in schools in Michigan, Montana, and North Dakota. In 1916, he enrolled in the University of Michigan at Ann Arbor, waiting on tables for his board and using money he had saved from work as a lumberjack for tuition. In 1918, he was graduated with a Bachelor of Arts degree and took some graduate courses toward a master's. He met Ethel Cora Eldred,[75] from Grand Rapids, Michigan, in a psychology class. Wilfred and Ethel married on August 27, 1918, at ages thirty two and thirty, respectively, and moved to Charlotte, Michigan, where he became principal of the high school.

In 1919, Wilfred quit teaching to take up farming[76] near Belmont, Michigan, where his first child, Lorraine, was born on July 21, 1920. But "the venture was unprofitable and unpleasant." Shortly after Lorraine was born, Wilfred and Ethel bought a farm near Caledonia, but "that venture too was unprofitable." This second farm was sold in August 1920. He took a position as

---

[74] An old term for kidney disease. Her death certificate lists Bright's Disease as the cause of death, but she also chewed snuff and Wilfred's daughter Eileen said she had mouth cancer.

[75] Ethel was born April 25, 1888, to Elmer Eldred, a farmer, and Emma (née Jones). Ethel graduated from high school in 1906 and in 1912 earned a Bachelor of Arts degree from Central College in Huntington, Indiana.

[76] Possibly on the Eldred family farm.

principal of a high school in Venice, Illinois, and his second child, Eileen, was born on July 23, 1922.

In 1922, he moved to Persia, Iowa, where he was principal of a consolidated grade and high school. His third daughter, Vivian, was born on August 31, 1923. That year he returned to Ann Arbor where he enrolled in the University of Michigan. He received his master's the same year. In 1924, he was hired to teach history at Morton High School in Richmond, Indiana. In 1924, he quit his job and turned to studying law. His son, Paul, was born on July 18, 1925.

Wilfred was admitted to the Illinois bar on November 5, 1927. He was a deputy prosecutor from 1927–1929 and also served as a judge for several years. After a time, he set up his own practice, which eventually failed, and he took a job in a factory. Despite his turbulent employment history, he still managed to put three of his children through college. Ethel died of cancer on September 30, 1950.

Wilfred spent his last years writing about logging, mining, and growing up in the Upper Peninsula. He died of a heart attack in a nursing home in River Forest, Illinois, April 8, 1966, just eleven days shy of his eightieth birthday.

Wilfred Nevue

Acknowledgements

My mother, Eileen Mae Lappe (née Nevue), had a fraught relationship with her father, Wilfred, so I am grateful she kept so many of his manuscripts, biographical notes, letters, newspaper clippings, and photos. Thank you to Rhonda Boshears with the town of Champion for the interesting conversations and for finding the school photo for me. A special thanks to Eileen Haavik McIntire, author of the 90s Club mystery series, for letting me pick her brain about publishing. And last but hardly least, thank you to my husband, Karl, for his editing comments, encouragement, and love.